Books by Don Durrett

A Stranger From the Past

Conversations With an Immortal

New Thinking for the New Age

Finding Your Soul

Last of the Gnostics

The Gathering

Ascension Training

Team Creator

The Way

The Path Forward

Get Healthy / Stay Healthy

America's Political Cold War

Post America: A New Constitution

The Demise of America

Spirit Club

Don Durrett

Copyright © 2010 by Donald David Durrett
All rights reserved.

Fourth Edition (September 2023)

Library of Congress Control Number: 2011920882

Cover & Book Design by EckoHouse Publishing.

ISBN: 978-1-4276-5069-6

www.dondurrett.com

Wisdom is knowing how much you don't know.

— Socrates

An unexamined life is not worth living.

— Socrates

Be kind, for everyone you meet is fighting a hard battle.

— Plato

Some of My Favorite Truth Bombs

A higher spiritual life is service to humanity.

Gratitude should lead to virtue, or else the gratitude is false.

Separation is a lie. We are not separate from anyone or anything.

What is true is always true.

Our beliefs and our intent create our reality.

Introduction

Soon, dramatic changes will begin that will lead to distress and disarray for millions of people. To say that our way of life is going to come to an end is an understatement. We are approaching a shift of epochal proportions that will lead to a new civilization. We get to experience the nascent beginning. In fact, we get to be the progenitors. However, getting there will be extremely chaotic. In fact, many will not survive the transition. If you make it to 2040, consider yourself lucky to be able to experience the birth of something amazing.

The information in this book will help you prepare. It is not a how-to survival guide, but a spiritual guide. For, this is a spiritual shift that the world is about to experience. We are going to shift from nearly everyone living with third-dimensional consciousness, to many living with fourth-dimensional consciousness. If that isn't weird enough, some people will disappear and go to the New Earth on the fifth dimension. If this sounds ridiculous, consider the multitudes who are expecting this shift. If you Google "fifth-dimension shift," millions of hits appear. Are all of these people delusional? No, they are not. I can tell you with near certainty, this is going to happen, and soon.

Those who affiliate with New Age groups or metaphysical spirituality are not as delusional as the mainstream media would like you to believe. This will be proven when the changes begin. The alternative healing modalities that this group has been perfecting for decades will keep them healthy. Many of these energy balancing techniques are considered foolish by the average citizen today. However, when people begin dying in large numbers from disease, this group will thrive. Holistic healthcare is only one piece of knowledge this group possesses. They also understand spirituality on a level that is beyond that of the average citizen.

This group's knowledge of the four levels of the aura – Physical, Emotional, Mental, and Spiritual – has brought them close to God. These are highly spiritual people with a close relationship to God. Once the changes begin, their Gnostic relationship with God will be revealed. People will be in awe of their knowledge and will hunger to understand it. Thus, to call them delusional is simply naïve. They are the ones who will be the new leaders of the coming new civilization. You can doubt me today, but watch what unfolds. They are the ones who have been students of archangels, such as Michael; ascended masters, such as St. Germain; and seventh-dimensional beings, such as Kryon. These discarnate souls have been preparing these New Age Lightworkers for this shift, and they are ready.

In the near future, new spiritual beliefs will be accepted that have little resemblance to what we base civilization on today. This book espouses, in fictional story form, those beliefs that will be the foundation of the new civilization.

Set in the year 2030, in the western portion of the United States, this story is based on the various sources I have studied and pondered. I do not rely on one source, or even one main source. I put all of the pieces together. Some of the sources I have studied include Nostradamus, Edgar Cayce, the Hopi, the Fatima Prophecy, the Mayans, P'taah, Kryon, Kirael, Chet Snow, Ruth Montgomery, the Great White Brotherhood, St. Germain, Bashar, Bartholomew, Abraham, Moria Timms,

Gordon-Michael Scallion, the Gulf Breeze Six, and various other channeled sources.

The vision for this book, however, is my own and will not be accurate. No one can predict the future. However, as we approach the shift, it is easy to see trends. Soon, the changes will begin, of this, I am sure. How soon? How intense? No one can know, but I am expecting a chaotic ride, to which this story attests.

On a positive note, when I originally wrote this book in the mid 1990s, I thought anarchy, rampant lawlessness, and an economic collapse were inevitable. Today, I am optimistic that these outcomes can be avoided and that the transition will be less dire than this book originally portrayed. Although, it is not going to be a smooth ride. Once we get to around 2025, life is going to be challenging for at least a generation. It will take four generations for the transition to be completed.

Donald David Durrett
September 2, 2023

x

Contents

Books by Don Durrett iii
Introduction vii
Prologue 1

Chapter One
   Trip to Bakersfield 5

Chapter Two
   The Park 19

Chapter Three
   Portland 27

Chapter Four
   Kidnapped for Breakfast 51

Chapter Five
   Spirit Club Begins 69

Chapter Six
   The Spirit Club Grows 99

Chapter Seven
   Denver 117

Chapter Eight
   Federal Task Force 133

Chapter Nine
   Final Spirit Club Meeting 151

Prologue

As I thought back to January of this year, 2030, I noticed that, even though a new year had arrived, people were not celebrating. In fact, most people believed it was going to get worse before it got better. And it was already *bad*.

I was not that surprised, because I had expected it to be bad. Yet, expectations and preparations can only take you so far. You still have to experience it. You still need to get up each day and remember how it *was*.

I remember what it was like at the turn of the century. Unemployment was under 5 percent nationally, inflation was nonexistent, and gasoline was only a buck and a quarter a gallon. In retrospect, America was at its height economically.

Who would have believed what would happen by 2030? Economic crisis, social chaos, martial law, state secession, and earth changes have all impacted our lives. Let's look at them one by one.

Economic Crisis. Whew! How could we have prepared for economic collapse? We discovered that the economic fundamentals we relied on were a mirage. The United States Government defaulted on its debt, which led to the collapse of the dollar and then to bank failures, one after another. The stock markets collapsed shortly after, and trading stopped. There wasn't a crash; there was a collapse. Companies that were household names closed their doors. Tens of millions of jobs disappeared. Most of the mighty corporations ceased to exist.

The economy, however, didn't completely collapse. Unemployment today is no longer measured, because there's no government agency to measure it, but it is approximately 50 percent of those who want to work. Maybe 20 percent of the population works full-time. Agriculture, energy, retail, and restaurants are the major employers. The basic industries that we need to survive are still around.

What has declined significantly are entertainment (professional sports, music, film, television), lawyers, policemen, and firemen. Government, finance, and consumer industries have languished. They exist in skeleton form only, nowhere near what existed before the collapse.

Consumer luxury goods are ignored by most. Nobody can afford a new car or a new computer, although used cars and used computers are still in demand. What's the point of using precious money for luxuries? Life is no longer about luxury. It's about survival – for yourself, your friends, and your family. Society is in retrenchment. Few people shop for new consumer goods, if they can even find them.

Life is not about new cars anymore. Today, life is about soap and toilet paper, not to mention a roof over your head and a full stomach. The few people who have prospered economically in these dire conditions have become pariahs. Capitalism and materialism are definitely unpopular, and those who flaunt their wealth are often robbed by thieves.

The vast majority have come to realize that we are experiencing the hand of God, and that God has revealed his opinion of capitalism and materialism. There is a feeling now that it is time to try something different. What that is, people have not yet decided. There is, however, a definite leaning toward a simpler way of life. People want life to be simple: God, family, friendship. Those seem to be the criteria most people use today.

The economic collapse is what changed everyone's perspective. Once jobs disappeared, people began to realize that we had to create a new civilization, and that our current way of life was no longer viable. The only option was to change our way of life. People began to think differently. As I mentioned, materialism and capitalism lost their allure.

Once this *new thinking* took hold, people began leaving big cities and forming small communities. Life became localized, with the Internet providing the only link to the outside world. People began working for local companies, eating local food, and socializing within the local community. Traveling became less common, and people stayed close to their communities.

Social Chaos. After the economy failed, society erupted into a frenzy that has still not subsided. First, there were riots and looting. That was followed by lawless anarchy. Luckily, the violence was concentrated in the larger cities. There is still rampant lawlessness throughout the country, but on the whole, most citizens have been law abiding. The smaller the city, the less has been the lawlessness.

There is no tax base to fund a police force, other than a skeleton crew. For this reason, it is dangerous to travel, not only from town to town, but even across town. In this kind of environment, safety is scarce. In short, life has become dangerous in many parts of the country.

Martial Law. Martial law was first declared in Chicago and Los Angeles. After that, martial law was declared in nearly every major city that had a large minority population: New York, Detroit, Atlanta, and St. Louis. Martial law still applies to most of these cities. In other words, once martial law was declared, it was never revoked.

What does martial law mean? It means civil rights no longer apply. It means that men in black uniforms with machine guns shoot citizens who confront them or dare to break the law. The big cities are war zones. Machine gun fire is as common in these cities as screeching tires.

Why would anyone want to live in the big cities? People didn't want to leave. It's their karma, I suppose.

But even though millions still remain in places such as Los Angeles, Chicago, and New York, most people have left the metropolises. Most of us have come to understand the futility of living in them. The wealthy who lived in the Los Angeles suburbs of Hollywood, Brentwood, Beverly Hills, and Malibu left long ago.

State Secession. Texas was first; Idaho, Montana, Alaska, and Hawaii quickly followed. Secession began shortly after the riots erupted. Texas didn't want the federal government taking over their cities. By the end of 2027, the United States no longer encompassed fifty states. In fact, state secession and economic crisis were the one-two punch that took the wind out of the United States Congress. Since 2027, Congress has existed as a powerless body.

Earth Changes. Whew! I knew they were coming, but my goodness! After 2020, earth changes picked up. Tsunamis, hurricanes, volcanoes, earthquakes, floods, drought, cold, and tornadoes forced millions to flee from their homes. The South, especially, was ravaged.

Since then, earth changes have been nonstop, and more and more severe. Every month, it seems as if a major event happens somewhere in the world. The earth changes are predicted to continue until 2035. A major tectonic shift is supposed to occur around 2037. California will become a series of islands. Nevada and Utah will be mostly submerged. Arizona, Oregon, and Washington will be partially submerged. A section of the Midwest will become an inland sea, stretching from the Great Lakes to a huge opening on the Gulf of Mexico. Omaha will become a port city, and parts of Louisiana and Arkansas will be submerged. The coastline of the East Coast will come inland. To say that this earth shift will be devasting is an understatement. Tens of millions will lose their lives.

Chapter One

Trip to Bakersfield

My friends and I were driving in the bobtail truck, making a road trip to pick up food in Bakersfield, California. Jeff was driving, with his son Kevin in the middle, and I was riding shotgun. The drive from Tucson had been uneventful, and we were looking forward to loading the truck.

"John, how many people are going to be at Bud's tonight?" Kevin asked.

"I don't know," I replied. "Usually, there are fifteen or twenty. Why?"

"Since we're getting close, I was thinking about it. I like sitting around and talking at Bud's. I always meet new people and learn new things."

I smiled at Kevin and nodded to acknowledge that I understood. Kevin was only nineteen. He and his dad, Jeff, were inseparable. Jeff and I were close friends, and we had been making this road trip for the last two years. We always came in late spring, and then twice in the summer.

Kevin was an old soul, like Jeff and me. He had been exposed to New Age knowledge and was comfortable talking about it. On our trips, the three of us talked quite a bit about spirituality. I respected Kevin and treated him as a close friend.

We pulled into Bud's parking lot. He lived on his farm near Arvin, a small town twenty miles east of Bakersfield. Bud farmed wheat, corn, potatoes, carrots, cantaloupe, and honeydew. He had fifteen hundred acres and sold all of his food directly to people at reasonable prices.

Bud was well known in the New Age community. He fed us. I came all the way from Tucson, but that wasn't unusual. People came from all over the state of California, as well as the northwest and the southwest. There was only one requirement to be able to buy from Bud. You had to be a New Ager.

Jeff parked in the dirt parking lot, along with the other cars and trucks. Bud had a large house with eight bedrooms. It didn't matter how many people showed up for the night. Everyone was welcome. If he ran out of beds, there were always sleeping bags.

Maria met me at the door. She spoke to us in her heavy Hispanic accent. "Mr. John, hi. How was your trip?"

I smiled, "No problems, Maria. Is Bud here?" Maria was Bud's helper. She was always cleaning or cooking. I had never seen her not working.

"Yes, Mr. John. He is in the den."

"Thank you, Maria. Do you know Jeff and Kevin?"

"Oh, sure. If you are hungry, there is vegetable soup, and it's delicious. Eat as much as you want. We also have Pyrenes bread today from Bakersfield."

We walked back to the den. It was a large room, approximately twenty feet by forty feet. This was where everyone gathered. There was a large-screen TV, and people were camped in front of it, watching the news. This was also where we ate, so chairs and tables were everywhere. Fifty people could easily fit in the room.

As I walked into the den, several people turned. Those who knew us rose in unison and came to give us hugs and

Chapter One - Trip to Bakersfield

welcomes. Everyone at Bud's house was a friend. We were like a big family.

I hugged Bud, smiled, and looked him in the eye. "It's good to see you. How's everything?"

He smiled. He was always emotional when we met again. "We're fine here. How are your wife and daughter?"

"Julie and Kate are fine. I've been working on another book, and it's almost finished. Life has been good."

"Come." He pointed the way. "I have some new friends who would like to meet you." Jeff and Kevin followed us.

We approached a group of people seated around a table.

Bud addressed the men at the table. "This is John Randall, the fellow I told you about."

One of the men rose and stuck out his hand. "My name is Adam. I've read one of your books. I sure would like to talk with you about it." He was tall, about six feet four, and wore a beard. His demeanor was gentle.

I shook his hand. "Sure, let me pull up a chair."

"These are my friends," Adam said. "We drove down from Sacramento today in two trucks."

I introduced Jeff and Kevin, and the three of us found a place to sit. Bud excused himself and left us alone.

"So, which book did you read?" I asked.

"New Thinking for the New Age."

"Ah, you went right to the deep stuff. I take it you enjoyed it?"

He nodded. "Very much. I really liked the chapter about the love frequency. I never really thought about it like that. Could you explain it to my friends?"

"Yeah, sure. But let's let Kevin have a go at it first. Then I'll fill in what he leaves out."

"All right," Adam said.

"All right?" Kevin asked with dismay. "As if I know where to start?"

"Come on, Kevin," I said. "You can do it. Just let it flow."

Kevin paused to reflect and then began. "The key to obtaining a love frequency is gratitude, but it must be authentic. You must show your gratitude by accepting everything that happens in your life as either a blessing or an opportunity. Thus, you should welcome everything that happens in your life and embrace uncertainty.

"This high level of gratitude, in tandem with trust that life is perfect, will change your frequency, which is actually a tone, to emit love and light. Thus, you become a light worker, and spread love and light.

"What we are really doing is aligning with our higher self, which is love and light. We are bringing our higher self down to this plane of existence, and this is possible through gratitude and trust.

"Of course, this can't be done if the ego gets in the way. So, you have to live in the present moment, with your mind quiet. You have to be an observer with your soul, which observes your thoughts, and keeps you grounded in the present moment. So, you use your soul to harness your ego."

Kevin paused and looked at me. "That's all I can think of."

I smiled. "Okay, but I know you can say more. You did a good job, Kevin. So, let's see," I said to Adam and his friends. "Love is more than a romantic connection between two people, or the love a parent has for a child, or love between siblings, or between friends.

"Love is much more powerful than people realize. Love is powerful because it is the core of our soul. It is also our connection to God, and it is our connection to one another. When we love someone or when we love ourselves, we are

Chapter One – Trip to Bakersfield

on the same wavelength as God. This is why, in Corinthians, Jesus said, speaking of faith, hope, and love, that 'the greatest of these is love.'

"What we are doing here on this planet, the meaning of life, is remembering that we are God. And the best way to remember is to get as close to God as possible. When we love ourselves and others, we are connecting to God. We need to fall in love with ourselves and others, and that's how we get close to God. Then love will flow in our lives, allowing harmony and joy to manifest. If we love enough, then the grace of God will become apparent.

"Love is the key to spirituality. Love is the key to everything. Why? Because love is the energy of God. It is literally the spirit of our souls. It is who we truly are. When we take everything else away, our personalities, our intelligence, our experiences, and so on, we're left with divine spirit, which is love. This is why when we love someone or love ourselves, it is the best feeling we can possibly have. Love is the ultimate. It is the Holy Grail. It is what leads us back to God.

"For this reason, the most important thing we can do is love. More specifically, the most important thing is to be *in* love. We need to be in love with ourselves and with humanity. The next most important thing is to recognize that everyone is divine and is a perfect manifestation of God. And because everyone is perfect, there's nothing to achieve or do. Consequently, if there is nothing to do, then all that's left is to be in love.

"So, since love is so important, obtaining a frequency of love should be our goal. And then once we achieve it, we can then spread love and light in everything we do."

I paused to get their reaction.

Adam thought out loud. "You're saying that life is about *being*, not about *doing*. All we have to do is be the frequency of love, and we will spread love and light."

I nodded. "You can't do something to create love. And because love is the doorway to God, it doesn't matter what you do in life. What is important is to *be* love. Does that make sense?"

Adam squinted his eyes. "I think so. You're saying that if we want to find God, then we have to be in love with both ourselves and humanity. And that without love, we'll never find God."

I paused. "Actually, it's easy to find God. I teach people how to find their soul all the time, which is an individuation of God. But finding your soul is only the starting point. You then have to marginalize your ego to obtain the frequency of love. That's the hard part, but that's another conversation."

"So, what you are saying," Adam said, "is that obtaining the frequency of love is not easy?"

I nodded. "No, it's very difficult and takes a lot of spiritual work. The ego is not going to play nice-nice, and let you suddenly love yourself and everyone else you encounter, and let you live in the present moment with the ego relegated to being silenced."

Everyone laughed.

I rose. "I'm heading for the soup. We can talk later," I said to my new friends. Adam nodded.

Kevin, Jeff, and I walked to the kitchen. We found a huge pot, bowls, and spoons on the stove. We also found bread and water to have with the soup. We served ourselves and then found an empty table where we could eat our food. There were about fifteen other people in the den. Soon the crowd would form a group and talk. This is what Kevin had been waiting for. This had become a custom because so many

Chapter One - Trip to Bakersfield

people had begun living in groups during the last few years. When people left their homes and headed for safer areas, inevitably they ended up living in small groups.

Bud came to our table after we finished eating. "John, when are things going to get better? Every day, I get calls from people who need food. It's amazing how much desperation is out there. It's getting harder and harder."

"Don't worry, it will get better soon," I said. "Yes, we're going through hardships, but we are also making major advances spiritually. It's just a matter of time before love begins to flourish. My estimate is that it will be in a few short years, as so many have forecasted.

"Bud, you and I have to be strong. We are the pillars. We provide the support that people need. It's people such as you and me who will make sure that love conquers fear. As difficult as it will get, we must persevere. We must have courage."

"I'm a pillar, huh?" Bud said. "It sure doesn't feel that way." Bud was a farmer, not a New Ager.

"Bud, why do you support us?" I asked. "I've often wondered."

"My daughter, Kelly," he mused. "After she died, I felt a loss inside that wouldn't go away. Then, a New Age friend of hers came to me asking for food. That started it. This is what Kelly would want me to do. So, I decided to help her friends. It gives me peace of mind."

"Which friend," I asked.

"Her friend was Joe Bishop."

"Joe Bishop? How much food did he ask for?" Joe Bishop had a huge New Age community with over a thousand people north of San Francisco.

"Well, he knew I had a big farm. When I said that he could have whatever he could pay for, he asked for five truckloads. He still sends a truck once a month."

"Hey," Kevin interrupted, "people have begun to form a group across the room. Let's go join them."

We got up and moved closer to the group that was forming. As usual, the first topic discussed was politics, or something to do with local government.

A man in his early twenties was speaking. "Something has to be done to stop the crime. I don't even like to drive across Bakersfield anymore."

"Embrace the uncertainty. Embrace the perfection," I said. "What's happening is chaotic, but it's still a blessing from God. When we believe and trust in our own divinity and our own eternalness, there's nothing to fear and nothing to worry about. Truth and fear cannot coexist, and the truth is that we are love. Fear is false evidence appearing real, and love *is* real. All we need to do is follow our path and shine our light, thereby sharing our love with the rest of the world.

"Kirael said that the most important person to love is yourself, because if you love yourself enough, you can share that love with others. That is wisdom we should all embrace. If you have enough self-love, you will love others too. And this love – this truth – will smother any fears that enter your mind."

"Is it really that easy?" asked a lady with long, light brown, curly hair.

"No, it's not easy," I replied. "But if you get on a spiritual path and have enough trust in God's plan, then you can live in a state of love, instead of a state of fear. Also, if you want to help speed the transition, the best way is to shine your light and share your love. We don't need to form citizen groups, political groups, or get involved in politics. All we need to do,

Chapter One - Trip to Bakersfield

is love each other, and that's it. If enough people shine their light and live in a state of love, then we can change the world peacefully."

I paused and scanned the room. "Doesn't everyone see that fear is simply the lack of trust in God? If we begin to decide the fate of others by using politics and laws, then we're deciding out of fear. In essence, we're denying our trust in God. Our beliefs are implying that we don't trust God to fix the problem. We're implying that we need to create rules and laws to determine how people should live.

"The only reason we need laws is because we're afraid of what people will do. But we're entering a new era now, a new civilization. We no longer need to decide how people should live. Everyone is free to do as they wish. This is possible because love will flourish. And people who aren't of love will no longer incarnate on this planet, or be allowed in our new communities. Those who lack spiritual awareness can live amongst themselves until their generation slowly dies off. It will take four generations until the transition to love is completed."

"How do you know this?" a man in a bolo tie and cowboy hat asked.

"My name is John Randall," I answered. "I am a New Age writer. I've been doing research since 1989. Love will begin to flourish on this planet in the near future. Soon, fourth-dimensional consciousness will envelop this planet, and a new civilization will arise. Look around at the changes that have occurred in the last few years. Anyone can see that something new is going to arise from the economic and social chaos. Do you really think we can go back to anything resembling the past?"

"No," he replied. "But I think we still need to have laws and courtrooms."

"Why?" I asked.

He hesitated. "I don't know. It just seems like we need to have some kind of law and order."

"Watch what happens in the next few years," I said. "The vibration of the mass consciousness on this planet will continue to rise. Love will spread from town to town, person to person. In the not too distant future, crime will be rare. What will happen is revolutionary, beyond our imaginations. When love replaces fear, which is still dominant today, we, as a people, will no longer require written laws or courts of law. Instead, we will have agreements. We will agree to love each other and trust each other."

"And in the interim?" he asked. "We just allow lawlessness? We just love?"

"I know it sounds strange, but yes, that's my suggestion. The reason for this is that we transmute fear with love. Fear begets more fear. War begets more war. People who inflict their will on others do so out of fear. If we react to their fear with our fear, then we only compound the problem ... if it is a problem."

A lady sitting next to me asked, "What do you mean? Do you think the current lawlessness is okay?"

"Everything is a perfect manifestation of God. Everything happens because it's supposed to happen." I gestured with my hands. "Let me clarify. This is kind of complicated, so bear with me. There are no accidents, and there are no victims. Nothing happens to anyone unless they create it or co-create it. If we are victims of lawlessness, then we co-created the experience with the perpetrator. Thus, we are as responsible as the perpetrator.

"That may sound a bit bizarre," I continued, "but we are much more powerful than we perceive ourselves to be with regards to manifestation. The reason is that *we* are aspects of

Chapter One – Trip to Bakersfield

God. In essence, we *are* God. The ramifications of this fact are rarely understood in society today."

"I am an old soul," I added, "and I have done a lot of research about God and who we are. I write books about it. There are some truths that are universal, and are in fact, objective truths. For instance, all is perfection, and all is God. The reason why is because there is only one consciousness, which is God. We each share this interrelated consciousness.

"Once you recognize this truth, you will be true to yourself by loving yourself, since you are God. This will then extend to others. Eventually, you will no longer abuse yourself or others. Instead, all you will feel is love, which you will want to share. You will become harmless to both yourself and to others. Even more than that, you will become a positive aspect of God. Right now, most of us are negative aspects. Instead of helping the planet evolve, we are holding it back. As the saying goes, you are either fixing the problem, or you are part of the problem."

The group was silent. Kevin smiled. He was always amazed when people heard the truth for the first time. "Makes your head spin, doesn't it," Kevin said to the group.

"Yeah, it's a lot of information to absorb," one of them responded.

A man from the Sacramento group asked me, "Could you leave some of your books with Bud the next time you come?" He was short and stocky, and it looked as if they brought him along to drive the truck.

I smiled. "Sure, we'll be back this summer. I'll bring a few copies on the next trip." I got up.

"No, don't go," he said, raising his hand. "Can we talk a little bit more?"

I sat back down. "Sure."

"I've heard before that we are God," he continued, "and that we all share one consciousness, but I've never been able to understand how it affects my life."

I pondered for a moment. "When you were a child, you were likely told that God was in heaven and that He decided who was worthy to join Him. Thus, from childhood, you held the fear that you were potentially unworthy of God. The result was a hole in your heart, a chasm. This chasm caused you to judge yourself to be potentially lacking and unworthy. When you judged yourself to be potentially lacking, you created a separation between your true self and who you perceived yourself to be. This judgment of yourself was the basis of your current Earthly identity. You thereby separated yourself from God, which is your true self.

"You have been conditioned from childhood to forget who you truly are, and you have forgotten. When you begin to remember, you will begin to heal the chasm, your broken heart. You will begin to love yourself. Once you love yourself completely, you will love *everything* completely. With this remembrance, you will slowly learn to not judge yourself, and to not judge others, because they are reflections of your true self. Ultimately, everything is one, and this recognition ultimately leads us to enlightenment. This is what we all aspire to attain."

I paused and scanned the room. "If you want to create change, the best way is to embrace everything in your reality as perfection. Embrace everything with the understanding that you are co-creating the events in your life, and so is everyone else. Embrace life and allow it. Embrace uncertainty. Embrace whatever happens in the present moment. Why? Because what we resist, persists. What we deny, we give power to over us.

Chapter One – Trip to Bakersfield

"What we attempt to control with our judgments, we empower. There is no reason to try and make things better by creating new laws. In fact, that is counterproductive. The key is to be. There is nothing to do, except to *be*. Be love. That's it. Everything else is a trap that eventually leads us to love. You can either understand it now and help the planet evolve, or you can be part of the problem that forces the rest of us to solve."

"Are you implying that we don't need to rebuild society?" asked the short, stocky man. "That all we have to do is live in love and let what happens happen?"

"Exactly," I said. "Look around. Look at what we've wrought. It's time to let God show us the way. We don't need to solve any problems, if there are any problems. God can manage. Trust me, the world is in good hands. Our role is to get out of the way and let God show us what love can provide. If we love each other, God will manifest a harmonious civilization."

"All we need is love? Is that what you're saying?" asked the short, stocky man.

I nodded. "And trust, lots of trust."

"If there is nothing to do, then why do you write spiritual books to awaken people?" asked someone in the group.

"That's a good question," I said. "I write because that is what my heart tells me to do. We are all here to play a role of some kind. The key is to figure out what your role is. When I say there is nothing to do, only to be, I am talking about following our hearts.

"In the old paradigm, we were always trying to achieve or sustain a certain standard of living. The old paradigm was about doing. We were always doing things to achieve or attain something. In fact, achievement was probably society's highest accolade, and nearly everyone wanted to achieve something to feel important or special. However, when I wrote my books, I didn't write for the accolade. I wrote because that is what I felt compelled to do. I was *being* as much as I was *doing*. Does that make sense?

"When we do what others expect of us, that is different from doing what we feel compelled by our hearts to do. Following our hearts and doing what we most want to do. That is being. That is playing the role that we came to play. That is how we enjoy life, and how we follow the love in our soul. Trust your heart and follow it. Your soul is trying to tell you where to go. Just make sure you are listening to your soul and not your ego."

I stood up, "Okay, that's all I got tonight. It was a long drive. Time for bed."

Chapter Two

The Park

The next morning, Jeff, Kevin, and I loaded the truck and headed back to Tucson. We arrived without incident in the late afternoon. Julie, my wife, and Samantha, Jeff's wife, greeted us. We had lived next door to each other for nearly a year now and had become close friends, actually more than friends, an extended family.

We lived with a group of approximately one hundred people. I say approximate, because the number changed from week to week. People came and went. It was not unusual to meet a new face or say goodbye to someone who was moving on.

The majority of the group lived in twenty houses next to a park. We also used a section of the park as an additional place to live. It had tents, showers, restrooms, and an area where people gathered to cook and eat. In the park, we also had a large garden, a garage to fix our cars, and a healing center.

All members of the group were New Agers, which was our criterion for membership. People who wandered into the park didn't mind moving on when they found out that we were all New Agers. Most people didn't want to live with us. We were considered strange by some and a cult by others. Some people asked if they could stay and learn about our beliefs. We were delighted to have them stay.

We occasionally had infiltration issues with homeless wanderers. We would inform them that our community was private, and that they could not stay. Then we would feed them and give them a ride across town if they would not leave.

Nearly a third of the group had regular jobs in Tucson or another town nearby. I worked as the manager and owner of a family-style restaurant that served breakfast, lunch, and dinner. I went from being a software engineer to a restaurant owner. I figured people would always need to eat. I liked my new job. It was easy, and I got to interact with the public. I also had the opportunity to provide jobs for people in our group.

Two-thirds of our group were unemployed. However, that didn't mean they weren't active. Everyone was productive, and there was plenty to do. For example, people worked in the garden, made clothes, scavenged for necessities, cleaned, and fixed problems in the homes. There was always work to be done.

Our group was not that unusual. People had been living in groups since 2027, when the U.S government basically declared bankruptcy and defaulted on the national debt. Once government checks stopped flowing, many people had no choice but to abandon their homes and apartments. In the Tucson area, hundreds of small groups lived together. This was common throughout the country.

I got out of the truck and hugged Julie and Samantha. Kate, my seven-year-old daughter, was also there to greet us. I picked her up and hugged her. "How are you today?"

"Fine. Mom and I are making leather belts for the swap meet. Do you want to see them?" Kate was mature beyond her years. She talked as if she were a young adult. I no longer was amazed at the things she said.

"Yeah, let's go look at them."

Chapter Two - The Park

Julie and Samantha loved to make crafts that they could sell at swap meets. They taught and inspired each other and made an array of creative things.

"Your agent called," Julie said. "He expects you to speak at the Expo in Portland next month, then Denver in August."

I nodded. Stan Davidson was my lifeline to my other job, which was writing and speaking. He did everything for me when it came to publishing. I gave him my books, and he had them edited, published, and distributed. In return, I promoted them and shared the profits.

Julie didn't like for me to travel, and I didn't blame her. In these difficult times, she didn't want to be separated from me for long periods. But she accepted it. She knew how important it was to me. She didn't travel with me for several reasons. First, it was dangerous. There were a lot of desperate people who had turned to crime. Also, she needed to take care of Kate. It was better that they both stayed home. Lastly, I wanted Julie to keep our tent occupied and maintain a strong commitment to the group. I wanted our presence felt.

The belts that Kate and Julie had made were beautiful. They were handcrafted out of leather, with intricate designs, chiseled with a hammer and stamping tools. I wanted one for myself but didn't say anything. Julie and Samantha worked hard to sell their crafts, not to give them away. As I looked at their batch of belts, I said they were very nice, tempering my enthusiasm to own one.

Tomorrow was Sunday and the day of the swap meet. Kate would go with Julie and Samantha. I rarely went along. I worked either at the restaurant or with the group.

"Kate," I asked, "are you looking forward to getting a new book tomorrow?"

"Yes, I want another Harry Potter."

Julie always bought Kate a used book at the swap meet. They were only a dollar or less, and Kate loved to read them. She usually read every day. She got that from me. I read every night. From the time Kate was born, she had always seen me sitting in my chair or at my computer reading.

Julie and I decided not to send Kate to a public or private school. We would teach her ourselves. This was becoming more and more common. Society was changing so rapidly that organized schools were losing their significance. In fact, many public schools had closed due to a lack of funds. Those that remained were perversely overcrowded.

Today, homeschooling was becoming the norm. For instance, not one child from our group attended a school. In many respects, the schools that existed were an anachronism. Schools were antiquated and had not changed along with society. They taught students the curriculum of the past, which had little relevance for the future where we were headed. I foresaw schools soon disappearing in their present form. Education would go through revolutionary change, like the rest of society.

"Okay, time to unload the truck," I said to Jeff and Kevin.

The three of us went to find a few helpers. People were expecting us with a load, so it would be easy to find volunteers. We walked among the tents that were disbursed in small groups throughout a section of the park. Most of the tents were located underneath shady trees. It was early summer and hot. As we walked through, most people were sitting in the shade beneath the trees. We stopped occasionally and chatted. We always said hello to anyone we encountered. As we made the rounds, about ten people volunteered to unload the truck.

We emptied the truck at three locations: a garage at one of the houses, a storage tent near where we cooked and ate

Chapter Two - The Park

as a group, and the restaurant. I charged the restaurant a huge delivery fee that included the gasoline cost. It was so expensive that the restaurant barely made a profit. I wasn't sure how much longer I could afford to make the trip.

After we finished unloading the truck at the restaurant, we headed back to the park to eat. Everyone ate at the same place, which we called The Galley. There were usually people sitting in that area throughout the day.

Charlie would usually be around to help us find something to eat, no matter the time. Everyone called him Captain because he had once worked as a merchant marine and liked to wear a sailor's cap. He was in charge of The Galley. He was head cook and head organizer. He had helpers, but Charlie was in charge.

At the three main meals of the day, people gathered at The Galley. We ate in waves, and there was no specific time when we had to eat. If we needed to talk to or find someone, the best times were 8 a.m., noon, or 5 p.m. At those times, there was always someone eating the captain's grub.

Jeff, Kevin, and I approached the food line with the guys who had helped unload the truck. Because it was Saturday night, we were in for a treat. Charlie always baked bread and made a salad on Saturdays. Occasionally, there was even dessert.

As the line moved forward, I looked around at the people already seated. I waved and said hello to many friends. Julie and Samantha were seated nearby. I was content, actually happier and more satisfied with life than before the intense societal changes began. The reason why is because the spiritual aspect of my life had become more tangible. I felt more love being shared by humanity today. Not only that, but I also felt confident that this new flow of love would lead to something positive. I had become optimistic about the future.

Something good is going to happen soon, or at least by the time Kate becomes an adult. All we need to do is to allow the future to unfold. Not to do, but to allow. Not to strive or organize, but to be gentle and nurturing. We need to embrace today as perfection, rather than to judge today as lacking, or to try and do something about it.

It was not yet time to begin reorganizing society. It still had a way to fall. In fact, it would be counterproductive to begin reorganizing. In order to begin anew, we had to let the old fall away. Yes, many social structures had fallen, but beliefs were still in the process of transforming. Until the process was completed, society couldn't be rebuilt. In essence, it was a period when people were learning new beliefs, which was not an easy thing to do.

Jeff and I went and sat with our wives.

"Are you guys all done?" Samantha asked.

"Yeah," I said, "everything has been unloaded. It was a good trip."

"Speaking of trips," Samantha said, "before you leave for Portland, there's going to be a political rally downtown next week. I think it would be great if you spoke there."

I grimaced. "You know I don't want to." The political rallies were monthly gatherings in downtown Tucson. People got together and anyone could speak at the microphone. It was like talk radio, where anyone could voice their opinions. Samantha usually attended.

"I know," she said, "but you have something to say. I get tired of listening to fools."

"They are not fools," I said. "Everyone has their own points of view, and those perspectives are just as valid as yours or mine. Go and listen to what the people have to say, and keep an open mind. My point is to try to acknowledge that their points of view are valid, even if you disagree."

Chapter Two - The Park

Samantha gave me a cool stare. "John, you don't need to give me a lecture."

"I'm sorry, Sam. I have a habit of saying too much. Anyway, I don't speak at political rallies because I'm a spiritual teacher. Those gatherings are about politics, not spirituality."

"Yes, they are about politics," Samantha replied, "but I still want you to spread your message so that more people will wake up. I find it troubling that you don't speak in Tucson. How can someone with your knowledge keep it to himself?"

I hesitated. "That's not true. I'm constantly teaching. I write books, and travel, and do lectures at expos. I'm quite satisfied with my service to humanity. I have thought of opening a school, but if I do that, I'd have to give up the restaurant, which I don't want to do. I like being a common man and interacting with the public. I like sharing experiences with others and staying in touch with people."

"I'm sorry," Samantha said. "I get caught up with my own selfishness from time to time." She laughed. "I like to tell people how to live their lives. Sorry."

"No problem," I replied. "Just remember not to think with your mind, but instead with your heart. Forget about logic. That's the ego. Always think with love and feeling, which comes from the heart. Remember, the essence of love is *allowing*. In other words, allow me to live my life as I choose. Conversely, I will allow you to live as you choose." I looked at Samantha with a plea for forgiveness. "Did I say too much?"

"No, that was a good lecture. I'll try to stop bossing people around."

Everyone laughed.

Spirit Club

Chapter Three

Portland

Two weeks later, I was on a bus traveling to Portland. Air travel had been an option, but expensive, and I didn't mind the bus. It was a twenty-hour trip from Tucson to Portland.

I was alone. The bus had just pulled out of the station, where I had said goodbye to Julie, Kate, and Kevin. Kevin had asked to come with me, but Jeff and Samantha refused to pay the fare. I understood their decision. A round-trip bus fare to Portland was more than one month's living expense.

The bus was half full. I sat alone, next to a window, and read my notes. The desert landscape of short mountains, dirt, brush, and cactus swept past. I enjoyed these long bus rides. They gave me a chance to relax and think. Often, I wrote. I did some of my best writing on the bus.

It was early in the morning, so I would have daylight all day. I was looking forward to reading a new book I had recently obtained and reviewing some notes for my lecture. The book was channeled by Lee Carroll, from an entity named Kryon. I had read other books by Kryon and was certain that I would enjoy it.

My notes were on the topic that I planned to talk about at the Expo: ego and judgment. I read my notes carefully and filled my short-term memory. I knew from experience that I could improve my speeches by preparing diligently.

Yes, I could do the talks without preparation. I had enough knowledge to just show up and start talking. However, if I prepared, the audience would get more out of it.

*****

The bus pulled into the Portland terminal on schedule. Angie was there to greet me. We had met several years ago at another Expo in Portland, and I always stayed with her when I was in town.

"Hi, John. How was the trip?" she inquired.

I smiled. "No problems. How are you?"

"Great. I decided to pick you up when the bus arrived. I didn't want you to be stuck trying to find a taxi at 5 a.m."

She started walking to her car. I walked alongside her with my bag. "Thanks," I said.

We got into her car and headed for her house in Hillsboro, a suburb outside Portland.

"It's good to see you," I said. "Is Jamie still living with you?" Jamie had been her roommate the last time I was in town.

She nodded. "Yeah. She wants us to go to dinner one night while you're here. I told her that we would."

"Sure," I said. "Are both of you working the Expo?"

"Yeah. I'm speaking on Saturday and Sunday. And Jamie has a booth for her art. So, she'll be busy."

Angie was an expert in the field of energy healing. She had published a book and was nationally known. She was a frequent speaker throughout the country and was on the road more than me.

It was Thursday morning. The Expo would begin tomorrow, although I would be attending only Saturday and Sunday. I planned to take the bus back to Tucson on Monday morning.

Chapter Three - Portland

I always looked forward to the day before an Expo, when I could visit with friends. In each city where an Expo was held, I had several friends. I would call a few in the morning and find out where we would meet.

"Angie," I asked, "what are your plans for tomorrow?"

"Steve Strong is having people over to his house. I'm going there in the morning. Want to come?"

"Isn't he a UFO contactee?"

"Yeah. He still has contacts. He does seminars and lectures about them."

"Which star system is the UFO from?"

"Arcturus."

We both grew quiet as she drove down the freeway. I was thinking about when a UFO would officially land. I knew it would be soon. It could be next week, next year, or in five years. But it would be soon.

"Do you want to come?" she asked again.

"Yeah, that sounds good," I replied.

* * * * *

The next morning, Angie and I went to Steve's house in Beaverton, about ten miles east of Hillsboro. We took a public bus. Angie preferred the bus whenever possible. Automobiles were steadily becoming a luxury that few could afford. Gasoline was expensive and rationed, and maintenance costs were exorbitant.

On the bus ride, I asked Angie about recent crime and violence in Portland.

"It has steadily worsened as the economy has fallen," she said. "But it's much better here than in other large cities across the country. I don't know why, but civil chaos never exploded here. We haven't had martial law declared or military troops."

"Maybe the Mt. Rainier experience calmed everyone down," I said. Mt. Rainier had erupted in 2026 and drenched Seattle in volcanic dust and soot.

Angie raised her eyebrows and made a face that implied deep thought. "That might have something to do with it. Volcanoes and torrential flooding definitely got everyone's attention. I think people are mellower today. The earth changes have changed our attitudes about life. People around here have come together as a community. Well, most people, not everyone."

"Are you afraid to ride the bus?" I asked.

"Sometimes. Whenever I go downtown, I get nervous." She paused. "I worry. I know it's not safe downtown, yet I constantly take the bus to shop. If you want good food, you have to go to the open market. I go at least once a month."

"With all the difficulties finding food," I said, "I find it amazing that the downtown open market has never closed. You'd think that people would have rioted and looted the market by now."

"I know. It *is* amazing. You can find fruit and produce down there every day. Yeah, the prices are high, but at least people are being fed."

The bus came to Beaverton, and we got off. After a short walk, we found the street where Steve lived. It was a typical American city street: cars stripped and laid bare, homes abandoned and boarded up, trash strewn here and there, lawns not mowed, weeds dominant, and flowers scarce.

Chet Snow answered the door. I was surprised to see him. We hugged and said hello. We hadn't seen each other in a couple of years. He had published a book in 1989 entitled *Mass Dreams of the Future*. In the book, he was hypnotically progressed into the future. His vision of the future didn't turn out to be true, and neither did many other prophecies. Neither

Chapter Three - Portland

did Dolores Cannon's book *Conversations With Nostradamus*. What we learned was that there are many timeliness, and as a civilization, we never know which one we are going to select. Thus, the future is fluid and unpredictable.

I introduced Chet to Angie, and we followed him into the house. Seated around a table with Steve were two attractive girls in their twenties. You could tell that they fit into this crowd by their tachyon crystal pendants and angel earrings. Steve noticed Angie and said hello. Being a good host, he introduced us to the girls. We sat and joined them.

Steve and one of the girls were talking about the decay of society and about how everything was getting worse.

"As Elan would say," I added, "that's one perspective. Personally, I don't see decay. I see rebirth in progress. I'm ecstatic about the near future. People are changing, and the world is changing. Yes, institutions have fallen and will continue to fall. But spirituality is on the rise. Just five years ago, few people understood what I was writing about. Now, many do. Not the majority, but that's only a matter of time."

I smiled and continued. "We're in the front row. We're experiencing and witnessing an incredible event: the birth of a new civilization. I have a hard time not being excited and passionate. I don't care about the difficult aspects of everyday life. It's the changes that are occurring that are amazing. Almost every day, I realize how wonderful it is to be alive at this time. This is paradise."

"*This* is paradise?" Steve asked with a tone of astonishment. "What about the danger, fear, and paranoia that is so prevalent today?"

I nodded. "Yes, it is. If you know what we are creating, then the mess is worth it. In fact, the negative experiences that are prevalent today don't have to be our own. Everything in life is a perspective. For this reason, happiness is a *choice*. In other words, we get to decide the meaning for everything that happens in our lives.

"In fact, this world isn't real. The language and definitions that we use are just ideas. And these ideas keep us from the truth. Our ego-personalities are fake. Everything is fake. We make it all up so that our souls can evolve.

"Danger, fear, and paranoia are self-created experiences. Nothing on this plane of reality is real. It's all an illusion. The physical plane is nothing more than an ongoing, created illusion. Ask a quantum physicist. He or she will tell you that everything is pulsing in and out of existence. Our bodies are vibrating energy at around 100,000 cycles per second. Nothing is static. Atoms, the core of matter, are constantly on the move. What's *real* is our divinity, which we carry within. Everything else is an illusion." I paused.

"Don't stop," said one of the girls.

I smiled and continued. "The meaning of life is not to create happiness in our lives. In fact, those who are the most evolved are not here to have fun. That's not why we came. Instead, it is to find our divinity and share it with others. Happiness is a choice, but enlightenment is a path. The prevalent focus of pursuing happiness comes from the ego. The reason why so many people focus on negative experiences, such as fear and anxiety, is because of the ego. But the ego is an illusion, too, just like the world we live in."

"You mean I'm not real?" Angie asked.

I paused in contemplation. "If you mean, is your personality as Angie real, then no, Angie is not real. Your perception that you are a separate identity as Angie is an illusion. Our personalities are illusions, contrived for this lifetime. In other words, we are all wearing masks. The true you is hidden, which is your true self.

Chapter Three - Portland

"If you have an NDE, you will get to meet your true self. Your soul consciousness will pop out of your body, and your soul intelligence will suddenly appear, free of the ego's influence. You will feel so joyful that you won't want to go back into your body. All of our fears, desires, and temptations will suddenly be gone. All you will feel is bliss and joy."

I continued. "We're real in the sense that we are eternal souls. It's the consciousness of our soul that is real. However, even though our souls are unique and eternal, this does not make us separate entities from one another. You may be called Angie in this life, but on the spiritual planes you are known by another name, and your personality is much different.

"We are all related and connected, and we affect one another. All parts make up the whole. God is *all* consciousness, and each of us is an aspect of God. When you asked, am I real, you're implying that you are separate from God. The correct question is, are *we* real?"

"Why is that the right question?" Steve asked, intrigued.

"Because *we* are God, and God is real. In other words, life is about God. This planet is God's playground, and we are the children. As I mentioned earlier, it's hard for me not to be excited lately. I can sense that something wonderful is happening. People are starting to get it. People are beginning to remember that they are God. That awakening is what this rebirth is all about."

"If life is about God," Steve asked, "is that why you said the meaning of life is to find our divinity?"

I nodded. "Yes, we are here to become aware of God, to become aware that everything is God, and everything is perfection. Once we have this awareness, we're enlightened. However, no one becomes enlightened in one lifetime. This is why I said that enlightenment is a path. Spiritual awareness is a slow, incremental process. This is what reincarnation is all about. Steadily, we learn valuable lessons, life after life. One lesson at a time."

I gestured with my hands. "All experiences are valid, because all experiences lead to spiritual awareness. Not just the experiences that we deem spiritual, but all experiences...."

Steve interrupted me. "If all experiences are valid, then there's no right and wrong."

"That's right," I replied, "although such a notion isn't easy to accept. Until we're aware that we are all one, we question the perfection of life. We question the choices that people make. Instead of honoring that people are learning from their experiences, we judge their behavior."

I looked at Steve. "All choices have ramifications. This is something most people would agree to be true. From this belief in ramifications, we assume that because some choices have negative ramifications, some choices must be wrong. For instance, when someone murders an innocent human being, we assume that their choice was clearly wrong. This is how our current civilization works. We believe that we can determine right and wrong. However, not everything is as it appears.

"The person who chose to kill another did it from the perception of separation. They *believed* they were separate from the other human being, when in fact, they were killing themselves, since all humans are one consciousness. Do you punish someone for being naïve? God doesn't, so why should we? Isn't the correct approach to show them that they made a mistake?

"The reason civilization is going through this difficult transition is because of the current focus on right and wrong, the belief in duality. This is what has led us astray. This is what creates war, conflict, hate, negativity, et cetera. However, God does not have duality, and thus neither do we.

In other words, all of God's creations are perfect, including their choices. However, people have refused to believe that we are perfect. Once we realize that duality is an illusion, it will gradually disappear. We will steadily become aware that we are eternal beings who learn from our choices, and that life is a process of co-creation. The concept of being a victim will lose its meaning.

"As a civilization, we are becoming more spiritually aware," I continued, "with past beliefs giving way to new ones. A new fourth- and fifth-dimensional civilization is rising. However, we have not gotten there yet. Today, people are still concerned with their identities – their egos. We are still thinking in terms of right and wrong, good and bad, happiness and sadness.

"For instance, if we aren't happy, we blame it on someone else. We still think that some person or some group has done something wrong to prevent our happiness. Soon, we will laugh this off and say, 'Your life is perfect. Get a grip! Quit blaming people and society for your perceived misery. Wake up to your divinity! Happiness is a choice, and your beliefs create your reality. So, change them if you're not happy.'

"Today, people actually believe that someone else is preventing their happiness, be that a person, a group, or an institution. From this belief, people reinforce their unhappiness by judging other people, groups, or institutions as the culprits for their unhappiness.

"Instead of living with love in their hearts and the awareness that they are divine, they live with frustration and judgment. Instead of being true to themselves, they lie to themselves and perform self-abusive addictive behavior. If there is one thing I would tell humanity, it is this: You are God, so start acting that way by being true to yourself.

Without honesty, there can be no trust. Without trust, there can be no love.

"Unfortunately, to be true to yourself, you have to find your soul. And for many, this is not easy, and must be learned. I'm hopeful that the majority of people will learn how to find their soul. That soul connection will allow them to live primarily from their heart-center, connected to their soul, and not primarily from their ego.

"The ego leads us astray, and the soul leads us to love each other. It's really that simple."

I paused. "I remember when I first started learning New Age concepts. I was stunned by their significance. I thought about how people imprison themselves with their beliefs. I thought about how people constantly reinforce their own unhappiness. It's all based on beliefs. In other words, people do it to themselves."

I looked at the girl next to me. "I remember reading Bartholomew. He said, 'Be selfish with your anger.' He meant, when we get upset, don't let anyone have our anger; be selfish with it. By not getting angry when we are upset, we transform anger into love. Conversely, by getting angry, we are rejecting our divinity. Thus, the lesson of anger is to become aware of our divinity."

"Whoa!" one of the girls said. "I just had an epiphany. As people become aware of their divinity and the realization that love is the core of their being, anger will lose its hold on them. Everyone will become loving beings with much less judgment. Society will become peaceful."

I smiled. "Exactly."

"I don't know," Steve replied. "There is a lot of fear out there."

Chapter Three - Portland

"Steve," Angie said, "that is what this great shift is all about. You need to have more faith. Peace on Earth has been promised to us."

The group talked for a couple of hours. It was an enjoyable experience, sitting around and talking to interesting people. Angie and I hugged everyone as we made our exit.

On our way back to Angie's house, we stopped by the downtown open market and bought some fruit. The pineapples were ten dollars each, but a bargain, so we splurged. I hadn't eaten fresh pineapple in more than two years; it was a rare find. At her house, we cut up the pineapple. The sweet taste brought a smile to my face. It was strange how simple pleasures took on new meanings. This experience was like the scene in the movie *Soylent Green*, where Charlton Heston ate strawberries that were impossible to find.

* * * * *

On Saturday, Angie and I took the bus to the Expo at Portland State University. The university was closed for summer break. In the autumn, it would open again for thousands of students. The University continued with a curtailed curriculum, and many extracurricular activities, such as sports, had been eliminated. This school, however, was fortunate. More than half of the colleges in the United States had closed in recent years.

When Angie and I arrived at the Expo, the atmosphere was euphoric. For many, this was the one event they looked forward to each year. It was an opportunity to feed the soul and to experience hope for the future.

Expos in Portland, Denver, and Phoenix were all similar. They were held in cities where civil unrest was somewhat subdued. At those Expos, the populace welcomed the event with open arms. There was little protesting, and those who attended were excited. Expos in other cities, such as Los Angeles, were sparsely attended. The popular speakers refused to go there because of the danger. Cities such as Los Angeles, New York, and Chicago were under martial law, and violence was everywhere.

There was always a sense of awe at the Portland Expo. People walked around with bright eyes and a sense of wonder. They recognized that something special was happening at these events. This was where the new spirituality was being born. To be a part of this birth was exciting and important.

As usual, I queued in the line for speakers. Other people were in another line for admission. It was early, and the Expo was just opening. Only a few hundred people had arrived. A continuous stream of people would be arriving throughout the day. The Expo charged two hundred dollars for a three-day admission pass, or one hundred dollars for a single day. This was a significant sum of money, even with the devalued dollar.

To give you an idea of the value, it would cost about fifty dollars for a meal at the family restaurant where I worked. The bus ride from Tucson was five hundred dollars. The bus ride today was ten dollars. A dollar was worth approximately 25 percent of its former value since the government had declared bankruptcy. These, however, are only approximations because many items and services had skyrocketed in price. Asparagus, for instance, was unaffordable because of shortages. Oranges, apples, and cantaloupe were very expensive, even in season.

If the Expos were affordable, thousands would attend. With the high admission fee, however, only those who truly wanted to attend would come.

As I waited in line, I noticed people panhandling for the admission price. This was painful to watch, knowing that they should be allowed to attend. Each of us, however, had

Chapter Three – Portland

only so many resources, and few of us could give away those resources and still live our lives. Today, I could give only a few dollars to two or three people, which I did while walking from the bus. After that, I had to say no.

Angie and I parted, and I headed for my booth. When I found it, I noticed that Stan had already set up. On the phone with him this morning, he told me the booth number and the number of books he was taking to sell. I would be doing a lot of sitting over the next two days, seated behind a table stacked with my books. Stan was always confident that we would sell over one hundred books, and he was usually right.

People would stop by the booth, then ask for an autographed copy when they found out I was the author. I didn't particularly enjoy this. I preferred to be in Arizona with my family. However, I had agreed to this arrangement with Stan and my publisher several years ago, deciding that three Expos a year were acceptable.

I found my booth and sat behind the table. Stan had stacked two hundred books in the corner. I would see him sometime during the day. Meanwhile, he had other writers and publishers to attend to. It wasn't unusual for me to see him only a few times.

I noticed a friend at a booth nearby and went to say hello. She asked if I was giving a lecture today, and if so, at what time. I told her one o'clock, and she said that she would attend. That made me feel good. I always preferred seeing a familiar face in the audience. Speaking in front of a group of strangers could sometimes seem demanding.

I went back to my booth and waited for customers. From then until one o'clock, I sold ten books and had several interesting conversations. The time passed quickly. There was always energy in the air, so the time seemed to pass faster than normal.

Then it was time to give my lecture, so I made my way to the lecture area. The classroom was shaped like an amphitheater. There were twenty seats in the first row. The rows became wider up the stairs towards the back. The last row was forty seats across.

The room was nearly full, with only a few empty seats. I walked to the lectern and spoke into the microphone.

"Hello, everyone. My name is John Randall. Thank you for coming. I prefer to have a conversation. So, if you have a question, raise your hand and a volunteer will bring you a microphone. There are five cordless microphones, and we can pass them around.

"Okay, a little about me. According to the Michael Teachings, I am a

fifth-level old soul, Priest-Scholar. In astrology, I'm a Pisces, with Cancer rising, and with my moon in Sagittarius. Using Science of the Cards, I'm a five of diamonds, jack of diamonds. My life path is a one. My purpose in this life is to help people become more spiritually aware and to help them prepare for the shift. I have spent many lifetimes searching for this knowledge, primarily as a philosopher. In this current lifetime, I'm disseminating what I've learned.

"My current level of awareness is at the point where I can almost sense a oneness with All That Is. I consider myself a fairly grounded person, with a high level of spiritual awareness. Being a Pisces, which is a mutable sign, I can relate with nearly anyone. However, my spiritual awareness does make me somewhat unique. One time, when I was younger, a psychic held my hand and gasped, 'My goodness, you're normal!' She'd never felt someone with my awareness who was so grounded. She was right. I appear to be average, a typical American. It's difficult for people to perceive that I'm different, that I am a fifth-level old soul."

Chapter Three - Portland

I scanned the audience, looking at the faces in the crowd. "Before I begin this lecture, is there anyone here today who is a sixth- or seventh-level old soul?"

I scanned the audience, hoping that someone would raise their hand. No one did. With less than 1 percent of the population at sixth or seventh level old soul, and only a few of this group knowing their level, I usually did not find many.

I continued. "Today, my lecture is on judgment and ego, two concepts that are closely linked. Spirituality is really very simple once we grasp the concepts."

I paused. "Let me rephrase that. It's easy to begin a spiritual path using these concepts; however, making progress is a whole different story. For instance, the concepts I will explain today may take you several lifetimes to grasp in totality. Understanding the concepts is one thing, but putting them into practice is something different, and much more difficult.

"Ego. How many of us have realized that our current life is based on a false ego? And that our ego is nothing more than a temporary creation that we chose for this lifetime. It was chosen for only one reason, because it was suited for what the soul needed to learn in this lifetime.

"The ego has two purposes. First, to create a personality that we can use to learn our lessons. Second, to trap us in the illusion that the ego is real.

"This second purpose, the ego takes very seriously. In fact, the ego will do everything that it can to block us from the soul. Its favorite tricks are fear, guilt, addictions, vanity, and pride. One thing to understand, the ego does not care about our well-being. If it can drive us to suicide, it doesn't care. It would rather die, than lose. And by losing, that would mean the soul won.

"To begin our spiritual path, we must recognize that the soul is real, and the ego is an illusion. We do this by finding out which one is more powerful, and which one is really in charge. This is easy to determine because the ego can only exist in the chattering mind, thinking about the past or the future. The soul can only exist in the silence of the present moment. Once you figure this out, the ego can be marginalized.

"If you silence your mind, your soul will appear. That is your power. The ego cannot function in the preset moment unless the soul allows it. Thus, the soul has the power and not the ego. The soul can quiet the chattering mind. The soul is more intelligent than the mind. This soul is wise. The soul is love. The soul is real.

"On our spiritual path, we want to keep the ego in its place, and we want the soul to lead us. We want to keep the chattering mind quiet, and the heart open. We want the soul to show us the way. This is our intuition.

"The soul is our higher self and is much more important than the ego. In fact, the ego is our hindrance. It just creates problems. The ego is what keeps us trapped into the belief that we are separate from God and separate from each other. But separation is a lie.

"The first step to spiritual awareness is recognizing our divinity, realizing that we are part of God and thus, eternal. This also entails understanding that we are perfect, and that everything we ever did was perfect. This step is realizing that God is perfection and that we are God, and not just us, but everyone and everything. As you can imagine, this isn't an easy concept to grasp." Several people nodded and laughed.

"So, connecting with our soul using the present moment to control our ego is the spiritual path that you want to take."

I smiled. "The isn't easy. Usually, we don't even think about it until we are old souls. Instead, the average person

Chapter Three – Portland

is content to let their ego control their lives, oblivious to their soul. Moreover, we don't really grasp it completely until we reach the seventh level soul stage, which is the final incarnation, when we reach enlightenment."

Someone in the audience raised his hand, so I paused and pointed toward him.

"Then what?" he asked. "What happens after seventh-level old soul?"

"It's up to you," I said. "You can start another reincarnation cycle or stay on the other side and not incarnate. There are many options. For instance, you could be a guide for someone who is incarnate. Or anything you can think of. The opportunities are endless. The primary difference between incarnating and not is that there's nothing negative on the other side. If you want to experience the negative, then you have to incarnate. Some souls don't want to experience the negative and, thus, never incarnate."

I paused and took a drink of water. "Okay. Without this first step of finding your soul and marginalizing your ego, the second step can't be accomplished. The second step is removing the lie of separation from your life. When you begin to recognize that there is only one consciousness that we all share, and that we are all one, then you can hold love for yourself and love for humanity. At that point, you can begin to share love with everyone you encounter. Once you are on that spiritual path, you will be getting close to enlightenment.

"This talk is not about *how* to accomplish these two steps. Only you can find your own answers. Also, the speed with which you find the answers isn't important. Everyone in this room will take his or her own unique path to enlightenment.

"Everything you do in this life helps you on your path. For instance, listening to a talk like this helps. So does not listening to me." A few people laughed.

"Words are just words. Most of you have already heard the words I'm saying today. If words alone brought us to enlightenment, it would be easy to attain. However, experience is how we reach enlightenment. That said, let me use a few more words." I paused and smiled, and the audience laughed.

"The first step to enlightenment is difficult because the ego is mighty. The ego fools us into believing that our lives have a *human* purpose. But a human purpose, like the ego, is an illusion. Earlier, I said that my purpose in this life is to spread spiritual knowledge. However, my real purpose is to *experience* God. The minute I think that I'm a special messenger sent by God to enlighten the masses, we all lose, because I become an egomaniac trying to help humanity.

"It's a fine line between serving God and serving the ego. Eventually, we come to realize that God doesn't need our help because all is perfection. However, once we get to step two and begin to live in a state of love, all we want to do is help humanity evolve spiritually. I'm sure most of you in this room feel this way." Many in the audience nodded. "There is nothing wrong with this. It is what leads you to enlightenment.

"We all have our roles to play. It's how we choose to experience them that determines how we learn our life lessons. It's all perception. We can play our roles any way we want. Each of us gets to choose how we learn. Again, our real purpose is to experience God. Everything else is an illusion. For instance, I can believe that my speech today is helping humanity. However, the truth is that I am using this illusion to find my way back to God, to become enlightened."

I continued. "*We* are eternal. We were created in perfection. Because we were created in perfection, nothing needs to be achieved. In other words, the only thing we need

Chapter Three - Portland

to do is *experience* God. From these experiences, we evolve. Everything else is superfluous, even humanity and the world in which we live. We worry about war, global warming, and running out of oil. All of these are meaningless backdrops. They are all illusions. We have lived for eons. It is only the development of our souls that matters.

"When we begin a reincarnation cycle, we select a role. For instance, I'm a Priest-Scholar. We use our roles to determine our experiences and to help us evolve. Note that evolving is natural. It is a by-product of incarnating."

I scanned the room. "As I said, my purpose in this life is to expose people to spiritual knowledge as a Priest-Scholar. Well, my purpose is nothing more than a by-product of my reincarnation cycle. My purpose came after the fact. My true purpose is to experience God.

"We don't incarnate to achieve something for the ego. We incarnate for one reason, and that is evolution of the soul. Nothing more, nothing less. We are simply here to evolve. However, this concept is alien to the ego. The ego demands that there be an *earthly* purpose. This planet is so dense, and most of us aren't aware of our divinity, that the ego has an easy time convincing us that our lives must have an earthly purpose.

"You may ask, how can our lives *not* have an earthly purpose? The answer is that we use the illusion of this plane of reality to evolve, but the illusion is meaningless. This is why civilizations rise and fall and why universes expand and contract. The material world is simply a backdrop, a façade, a stage. Only the evolution of the soul is important. Thus, there is nothing to improve in the world, nothing to achieve. For this reason, our platitudes for earthly achievers are often misplaced. The true achievers are often leading quiet lives of introspection.

"The question arises, why do we use a false reality of illusion to evolve? The answer is that we became bored learning lessons in a place of perfect harmony and knowingness. Eons ago, we decided to use our creative abilities and created a place where we could evolve in different ways. Thus, planets and universes were created. Currently, people believe that God created this planet. In fact, *we* did … with God's help. Kind of mind boggling, isn't it? Until one gets to be an old soul, this sounds like a fairy tale. Anyway, let's continue."

I paused and took a drink of water. "We are God, and we have the ability to create. With this ability, we started creating. Many people think that God created this planet and everything on it. Think again! Souls like us created it. We created the universe as a playground to learn. We created the ego as a way to forget our true selves, our true identity." I paused to let these ideas sink in.

"My head hurts," someone in the first row called out.

I laughed. "Yeah, I know what you mean. This planet is so dense that concepts such as these can't get through to our awareness. Yet we know they are true.

"Think about how you currently live. You may already recognize that your ego is in complete control of your life, with your incessant chattering mind dictating your choices." I grinned with genuine understanding, having been there myself. "The ego thinks that it is real. All of our fears and worries are from the chattering ego, and they are all illusion.…"

"Then what is the meaning of life?" a lady with short red hair asked.

"I've told you several times during my talk, it's the evolvement of the soul," I said. "For society, there is no meaning. Meaning and purpose for planets and civilizations were both creations after the fact. Before we began creating universes, we existed as perfect manifestations of God. Then we decided to create a few universes for new experiences. Once they were created, the purpose of the universes became an afterthought. The purpose of the universes or our planet is simply to allow new experiences so that the soul can evolve.

"Once this concept makes sense, then many other spiritual concepts also become clear. For instance: To know God is to live without judgment. To know our true selves is to realize the perfection in everything. Once we achieve this awareness, we no longer judge. Instead of judging, we live in a state of joy, a state of love and compassion. This is why evolved souls are selfless, gentle, and use loving kindness."

I paused and scanned the room.

"Why would we judge, when there is no meaning or purpose to human life other than to use our experiences to evolve?" I asked. "The answer is that the ego fools us into believing there is right and wrong. The ego informs us that everything should be judged as good or bad. Thus, most people spend their lives trying to define what is good or bad. Most people do not believe that they are divine or that others are divine, although this is changing.

"Buddha came to the conclusion that there is nothing to do. He sat under a Bodhi tree and realized that we are divine, that, indeed, there is nothing to achieve other than an awareness that we are God. Then he got up and told others the good news. Buddha's legacy is similar to that of Jesus. Both spread the word of love, compassion, and nonjudgment. Both told people that, if we become aware of our divinity, we will become more compassionate and loving. In other words, because God is compassionate and loving, we can also be compassionate and loving."

I took another drink of water. "Why do people become compassionate and loving when they begin to become enlightened? Because they realize that we are *all* God, that, indeed, everyone and everything is divine. The only thing that obstructs people from the awareness that they are divine is the ego. And it's only a matter of time before we remember that the ego is an illusion, although for many, that may not occur in this lifetime.

"To give our lives meaning is to remember who we are. Everyone will remember, eventually. It is inevitable. It might require one more life, or five hundred more lifetimes. Eventually, however, we evolve to seventh-level old soul. Ultimately, we evolve back to where we started."

Several people smiled.

A man in front raised his hand, and I pointed at him.

"Shouldn't everyone be trying to become aware of their divinity?"

I contemplated. "Once you reach the old soul stage, you will begin to realize that spiritual awareness has a reward. At that point in time, it then makes sense to become more aware of your divinity. However, until you are an old soul, it might not make sense to spend every day, which is what is required, trying to remember your divinity. For that is the last lesson. Once you remember and become enlightened, the reincarnation cycle is completed."

I took a drink of water from my glass. "Okay, so let's define judgment. Judgment is the designation of good or bad. And, if we are God, then there is no good or bad. This concept is difficult to grasp, just like the fact that there is no purpose for society. Why? Again, the ego refuses to acknowledge such a concept.

"I bring up judgment because judgment comes from the ego. Judgment is a viewpoint of the mind. Judgment is

Chapter Three - Portland

nothing more than the ego's attempt to make itself real. The ego is constantly judging right and wrong. That's how the ego tricks us into believing that our personalities are real. We don't realize that we are defining our identities through judgment. We don't perceive we are under the control of the ego.

"Until we reach the old soul stage, the ego is in control of us. As they say in commercials: I guarantee it. Until we can learn to think with our hearts instead of our heads, our egos are in control. Or, to be more specific, our chattering minds are in control. The secret to spirituality is to feel with our hearts and *not* think with our heads – our chattering minds. Get out of your head and into your heart.

"Unconditional love doesn't come from the logical mind, but from feeling. The scriptures state that God loves unconditionally. God loves unconditionally because God cannot judge God. God does not judge, God feels. Thus, life is about emotion. For instance, when babies are born, all they can do is *feel*. When you look into their eyes and they respond, they are feeling your emotions. Their logical capacities are not built yet. This is the reason they are innocent. They are born with love and trust. That is everyone's beginning. Notice that judgment is not part of a baby's consciousness. This is what we have to get back to. It is where we started – love and trust.

"Any judgment by the ego is, ultimately, a judgment of God, because everything is a reflection of God. Thus, when we are judging, we are invalidating God, and we are invoking separation. In other words, ego is the means by which we invalidate God. A good acronym definition for ego is Edging God Out. That is what we do with our ego; we push God out of our lives.

"Judgment is a game of invalidation. People judge others because they don't believe in their own divinity or the divinity of others. By invalidating others, they are also invalidating themselves. They judge, thereby allowing their egos to feel alive. In fact, judgment literally feeds the ego. We create a false identity and isolate ourselves from God. Again, note how the ego could care less about our welfare! The ego does not care about our well-being."

"What are you saying?" asked a lady in a bright blue dress in the front row. "That the ego is a false identity?"

I nodded. "Yes, the ego personality that we think is who we are is an illusion. Our true identities, our true selves, are not what we perceive. On this planet, our ego identities are nothing more than masks that we wear for our roles. When we invalidate someone using judgment, we are saying that their role is wrong or bad. We are judging the grand plan of God as imperfect. This is a simple analogy, but it helps us to understand that judgment is nothing more than invalidating the dignity and divinity in others."

I noticed an Expo volunteer waving at me from the back of the room, so I looked at my watch and realized that my time was up. Someone else was scheduled to speak in this room after I finished. I thanked the audience for coming and mentioned that if they wanted to talk with me further, I would be at my booth.

Chapter Four

Kidnapped for Breakfast

Monday morning, Angie and her roommate, Jamie, took me to the bus station. We hugged tightly in a group hug as we said goodbye. Their faces reflected a gamut of emotions: happiness that we had been together, sadness that the world was in a state of turmoil, and concern for the hardships that lurked around every corner.

The weekend had passed too quickly, but I still had a good time. The Expo had been an uplifting environment. I had talked with many old friends and met many new ones. Angie and Jamie had been great hosts. Now, on the bus taking me home to Tucson, I began to come down emotionally, since it was impossible to remain on the endorphin high that these Expos provided me. This was a normal occurrence. I usually felt somewhat depressed on the bus ride home from an Expo, because I used these opportunities of traveling alone to think about my life and the lives of those I knew.

Life had changed so much in the last few years. No longer was life simple. Now everything was intensified. For instance, saying goodbye this morning to Angie and Jamie was intense; greeting my family when I got home would be intense.

Another thing that had changed dramatically in society was crying. Now, people cried all the time and were much more emotional than a few years ago. I didn't cry (except when I watched movies), but I did feel anxiety from time to time. I got anxious knowing that many of my friends and family weren't happy. I knew that life was perfect, but that didn't alleviate my sensitivity to the pain of others. I was quite satisfied with my own life, and I felt fortunate. However, because of the contrast, I acutely felt the unhappiness of others.

Society had broken down and most people's lives had become a daily struggle. One of the hardest things to overcome was expectation. Until 2020, when COVID hit, we lived at the height of an incredibly materialistic society. People had it good and expected life to continually get better. From 1945 to 2020, America did nothing but get better, in materialistic terms. The economy grew, and store shelves were always full. Endemic shortages had not yet arrived.

I remember prior to 2020, when America was at its height economically (as measured in net wealth). If you wanted something, you went and got it. Where I lived, you could choose from an array of stores. If I wanted a TV, I could go to at least ten stores within a thirty-minute drive. The same principle applied to groceries, clothes, gasoline, and so on. And everything was still fairly affordable (although gasoline was at three dollars a gallon and becoming expensive). My weekly grocery bill was around fifty dollars. Electronics were cheap. (A Dell computer was five hundred dollars, a microwave 100 dollars, a twenty-seven-inch TV two hundred and fifty dollars).

After living in this materialistic utopia, with expectations that it would continue, it was difficult for people to adjust. And to make matters worse, few people were prepared for the changes that had occurred. Many people were stunned and in a mild state of shock from the changes. Others were angry. Only a few took them in stride, with equanimity.

Chapter Four - Kidnapped for Breakfast

Riding on the bus and watching the Portland suburbs pass by, along with the various military vehicles and soldiers, I felt the anxiety of the local residents. Few large cities had been spared military occupation. The federal government simply announced that under martial law, the military would be required to maintain order in cities.

The result of military occupation was a pseudo, ongoing martial law throughout the country. Searches and arrests of citizens were common. Many new federal detention centers were built. These centers were internment camps that held thousands of people who had been arrested in the last few years, many of them simply for protesting.

Most of the people arrested were from major cities, where rioting and lawlessness were pervasive. Even in small cities and towns, there was a feeling of being at war. Armed troops were everywhere.

A lady walking down the aisle of the bus stopped and looked at me. "Aren't you John Randall?"

I nodded. "Yes."

"Can I sit here?" she asked, pointing to the open seat beside me.

"Sure."

She radiated enthusiasm. She was very pretty, about twenty-five years old, with long, wavy red hair and blue eyes. "My name is Cindy. I saw you at the Expo. Did you sell many books?" She extended her hand after sitting down and we shook hands.

"Nice to meet you, Cindy. You saw me at my booth?"

"Yeah. And I heard you speak in Los Angeles a long time ago. I really enjoyed it. You're a good speaker."

"I'd rather be known as a good writer."

She grimaced. "You're too deep. I mean, your writing is never going to attract a big audience. I read one of your books once, and it took me more than a week to finish, and that's an eternity for me. I usually read a book in two or three days. You make people think too much. Life is hard enough as it is. Who wants to read a book that makes life even harder?"

I laughed. "Yeah, you have a point. My books do make you think. That's my style. Wasn't it Socrates who said that an unexamined life is not worth living?"

She smiled. "Yeah, but it's difficult to examine your life and survive at the same time."

I laughed. "True, and the big questions can be a challenge. Most people don't think the big questions even have answers, so they don't look."

She nodded. "I'm glad there are people like you who are spreading knowledge. The New Age movement is really helping the world, and life is going to get better. I can just tell."

"Yes, life is going to get better," I said. "This planet is headed toward its spiritual destiny, a destiny of love and awareness. We have only a few more years of turmoil. Then we'll have a new beginning."

"You mean the Goddess energy will come back? We'll begin to acknowledge that the masculine and feminine are actually equal?"

"Oh, yes," I replied. "It's very near. The feminine is already rising. I can sense it with the women who are becoming empowered. Women are the leaders and co-leaders of the New Age movement. Men are beginning to acknowledge the equality of the sexes. Changes are happening."

"Have you heard of Mary Magdalene being referred to as the Holy Grail?" Cindy asked.

"It sounds familiar...."

She became very animated. "I read about it in a book called *The Woman with the Alabaster Jar* by Margaret Starbird.

Chapter Four – Kidnapped for Breakfast

The author contended that Jesus was married to Mary Magdalene, and that she was pregnant with his child when he was crucified. Thus, *she* was the grail. She was the chalice that held the blood of Christ. Supposedly, she had a baby girl and raised the child in southern France. The child's name was Sarah, and Sarah began a legacy. Sarah had sons and daughters who carried the bloodline forward. Supposedly, they became kings and queens of France in early medieval times before the Crusades."

Cindy looked into my eyes to make sure that I was interested. I was, so she continued. "Sarah was widely known as Jesus' daughter in southern France, and a form of Christianity took root in that region, a form that was strongly metaphysical. This Christian faith was known as the Cathars' faith. It flourished for over a thousand years in southern France, until the Catholic Church funded the Albigensian Crusade to wipe them out as heretics. The Crusade lasted from 1207 to 1227. But before they were wiped out, they left behind evidence of their Gnostic faith."

Cindy became animated. "The Knights Templar were also from southern France. They were a wealthy, secretive, monastic order who came to be known as heretics for their Gnostic beliefs. Ironically, it was them, and not the Catholics, who built the first gothic cathedrals in Europe. In 1307, the Knights were tortured and killed by the French monarchy for heresy, and to confiscate their wealth. When the Knights were arrested, they had more wealth than any enterprise in Europe, other than the Catholic Church. They even had a fleet of ships.

"The Knights were only one of the groups from southern France that flourished with their own form of Christianity. There were others. The Troubadours also came from that region during that time and were known for their songs about a woman named Sarah.

Cindy spoke fast. "Artists and poets from this region also left an indelible stamp. They left behind many clues to their beliefs. But they had to use symbols because of the Inquisition and the threats of the Catholic Church. These symbols were very popular in southern France and exist to this day in European and Western cultures. The paintings and poetry in southern France from this period are quite convincing. The painters and poets believed that Mary Magdalene was Jesus' wife, and also that the beliefs of the Catholic Church were missing the feminine that she represented." Cindy finally paused to take a breath.

I had already read about the Knights Templar, Mary Magdalene, and the Cathars, but Cindy was so inspired that I let her speak as if this were my first introduction. I kept my mouth shut and let her continue.

"One of the fascinating things in this book is the prophecies from the Old Testament. They can be interpreted to imply that, until the feminine is restored, there will not be balance and harmony in civilization. The prophecies can be interpreted to imply that Jesus is the masculine and his bride, Mary Magdalene, is the feminine.

"It's quite fascinating to read the two-thousand-year-old prophecies and realize that they are about to transpire. The feminine is on the rise. We don't have to look far to see that men and women are working together to rebuild society. Changes are finally happening. Women are finally being viewed as equals."

Cindy stopped again and waited for me to speak. I smiled. It was exciting to meet someone as passionate about spirituality as myself. "I want to read that book," I said. "I'll try to find it."

"I'll send you my copy. Just make sure that you return it." She smiled.

Chapter Four - Kidnapped for Breakfast

"Thanks. I'll give you my address. Now, about these Cathar heretics. If the Cathar faith was flourishing in southern France, I would think that the Catholic Church was a bit upset?"

Cindy's eyes lit up. "Oh, yeah. The first Inquisition was instigated from 1227 to 1242 to remove the remaining Cathars after the Albigensian Crusade ended. The Cathars were Gnostic Christians who believed that one's spirituality comes from a personal relationship with God. They were known for meditating, being vegetarians, and some strange belief that the world was an evil place. They also didn't build churches, but prayed directly to God. The Catholics considered them heretics, even though the Cathars were extremely moral and lived ascetic lifestyles. One thing that is interesting about the Cathars is that they had both men *and* women priests. They were called Perfecti.

"From history, we know that, during the Middle Ages, the Catholic Church was a powerful political institution. The Church could do pretty much what it wanted, and it used its power to control and manipulate society. The Cathars were doomed for not abiding by Catholic doctrine. Their belief in honoring the feminine was their undoing. Having women priests walking around southern France was not acceptable, especially when the local people supported the Cathars more than the Catholics. Not to mention their belief that Sarah was Jesus' and Mary Magdalene's daughter!

"The Inquisition did everything they could to destroy the sacred feminine. All we can do today is analyze the clues of the past: the beliefs of the Cathars, the songs of the Troubadours, the poems of the writers, the paintings of the artists, the cathedrals of the Templars, and the legends and celebrations. To this day, southern France celebrates on May 24th for Saint Sarah in Saintes-Maries-de-la-Mer. And they hold Mary Magdalene Day on July 22nd in Saint-Maximin-la-Sainte-Baume. Both celebrations date back to the Middle Ages. They have been holding these celebrations for more than a thousand years!"

Cindy's eyes gleamed. "One theme that abounds in the clues is the value of the feminine. Whereas the Catholic Church was a patriarchal church that subverted the feminine, the Cathars and the Troubadours honored and revered the feminine. They understood that the masculine and feminine must be in balance. And today, the feminine side of spirituality is coming back."

I nodded. "I agree. Soon spirituality and religions will be based on equality of the sexes."

Cindy nodded. "The soul doesn't have a gender. The personality that we select for this lifetime determines our gender, and gender is basically irrelevant. No one gender is better than another. Equality is the true reality."

"It's interesting," I added, "that the Cathars honored the feminine at a time when the Catholic Church was setting the foundation for a patriarchal society. No wonder the Inquisition appeared to stamp out the feminine. However, their karma is coming back around. Notice how the Church has been losing its members the last few years? The patriarchal system, which the Church reflects, is being rejected."

Cindy pushed her hair back out of her eyes. "Yeah, I think Christianity is evolving into something completely different. My friends and family don't go to church anymore. They still pray, but whereas in the past they went to church and prayed in a group, now they pray as individuals, outside of any formal setting. Church no longer provides what people need."

She stopped and looked at me. "Why do you keep staring into my eyes?"

Chapter Four - Kidnapped for Breakfast

"I'm sorry. It's a habit of mine. I was trying to see into your soul."

"Hmm. What do you see?" she asked with a mischievous grin.

"A soul that is prepared for its journey and is getting a lot out of this life."

She raised her eyebrows. "I'll take that as a compliment. Well, I'd better get back to my seat. My friend is probably wondering what happened to me."

I reached into my wallet for a business card. "Here's my address for the book."

She reached for it and then stood up. "Thanks for listening."

I smiled. "It was nice meeting you, Cindy."

"Bye."

She turned and walked down the aisle.

* * * * *

Early the next morning, the bus pulled into downtown Tucson. No one was there to greet me. It was nearly dawn, and the moon still shone brightly. Julie was asleep, and I didn't want to wake her, so I decided to walk home. It was six miles, and the walk could be dangerous. I could have taken a taxi, but after sitting on the bus for so long, I relished the long walk.

I strapped my backpack over my shoulders and headed east. I figured I could walk three miles an hour. So, I would be home before Julie and Kate woke. A little exercise was just what I needed.

Travel by walking was popular now. Automobiles were a luxury that most people did without. I had met many people in Tucson who walked long treks. Walking all the way to Phoenix, nearly one-hundred and twenty miles north, wasn't uncommon. Walking across town was an everyday occurrence for many.

The city was asleep. I navigated the first few miles in the dark, walking at a steady pace along a main street. It was familiar. Many people slept on sidewalks and in alleys. After a few blocks, someone asked me for money as I walked past, but I kept walking.

The downtown streets were littered with trash and debris. The stores still in business were few, and most of the rest were boarded up. It was easy to imagine that the downtown area would soon fester into an abyss of degradation. The signs of this tragic fate were easy to see: graffiti, broken windows, broken stop lights, damaged road signs, and numerous potholes. The explanation for the degradation was simple: the city could no longer afford maintenance.

As daylight began to appear, I heard a rumbling of voices. Before I could avoid a confrontation, three men appeared in front of me. I had to stop because they blocked my path. They were dressed in tattered jeans and leather jackets. Each had long, disheveled hair, and more than a few tattoos. Not a crowd that I would have hoped to meet.

"Hey, Joe, what are you doing in our neighborhood?" one of the men asked in a threatening tone.

"Just passing through." I was afraid, but tried to remain calm.

"Where you coming from?" another asked.

"The bus station. I just got in from Portland."

"What were you doing in Portland?"

I hesitated, not knowing their intentions. "I was a speaker at the New Life Expo."

One of the men's eyes lit up. "What did you speak about?" This guy seemed to be the leader, and I could tell by their body language that the other men deferred to him.

Chapter Four - Kidnapped for Breakfast

"I write New Age, metaphysical books. I usually talk about what I have written. In Portland, I talked about judgment and the ego."

"You're coming to breakfast with us! My sister's going to be really excited to meet you. Come on." He motioned by leaning his head, and we all started walking down the street.

I thought about asking if it was all right if I passed on breakfast and went my own way. But I could tell that these guys were dangerous, and I wasn't about to press my luck. If they wanted me to go to breakfast, I was going.

It didn't take long to get to their house. It was in a neighborhood a few blocks from downtown. I hadn't been down there in a few years. As I looked around, I suddenly knew why. It was eerily in decay. Without garbage trucks running, it didn't take long for a neighborhood to degenerate.

As we walked along the street, I heard barking dogs. I knew that a dog could easily appear at any minute, as several of the fences were in bad shape. Now I was glad that I wasn't alone.

As we approached their house, the sun was rising. The temperature was already warm. It was going to be another hot day. I followed them across the gravel front yard and into the house. A broken down, dust covered Volkswagen Beetle was in the driveway. It had been there for some time, by the look of the flat tires and cobwebs.

Inside, at least five people were sleeping on the living room floor. I estimated that another ten were probably in other rooms. Few people were awake. We made our way gingerly past those who were sleeping and went to the kitchen.

The house was over three thousand square feet. The kitchen was large, with a big dining table and ten chairs around it. We sat down at the table, and one of the men began making coffee.

"What's your name?" one of them asked in a friendly voice. By now, they had all visibly relaxed. I had the feeling that everyone here was part of an extended family and that I had nothing to worry about. Plus, I'd seen women and children in the living room.

"John. What's yours?"

"Billy. This is Sam." He pointed to his friend. "And Charlie is making the coffee." It was Charlie who wanted me to meet his sister.

"How are you guys making out?" I asked.

"We're getting by," Billy said. "But when is it going to get better?"

"Let's wait for Charlie and I'll tell you." I implied that I *knew*.

"Whoa, man, you're scary," Sam said. "You know things, don't you?"

"Yeah. Sometimes I wonder why."

Charlie came back and joined us.

"Charlie, have a seat," Billy said. "This is John," Charlie extended his hand and we shook. "He wanted to wait for you before he told us some things."

"What are you going to tell us?" Charlie asked.

"Billy asked me when things are going to get better. I have a few ideas about the future, and I thought I'd tell you, if you like."

"Sure," Charlie said.

"I've been able to predict the future since 1999." I paused and let the statement sink in. "What has unfolded since then has not surprised me. The future isn't exactly predetermined. But, on the whole, the trends have been set."

"So," Charlie said, "you're going to tell us the future?"

I nodded.

"Okay, go for it," he said in a respectful tone.

Chapter Four – Kidnapped for Breakfast

"We are on the verge of a spiritual shift. Not just any shift, but a great shift. The planet is going to change from third-dimensional consciousness to fourth-dimensional awareness, and then some will experience fifth-dimensional awareness. This means peace on Earth is coming. More specifically, it means the end of our current reality...."

"The end of *what*?" Sam interrupted.

"Once enough people reach fourth-dimensional awareness, our beliefs will change. We will begin to recognize that there is no separation between anything and that we all share the same consciousness. We will become aware that we are all one.

"One of the first signs of fourth-dimensional awareness is heightened intuition and another is telepathy. Once enough people begin exhibiting these traits, society will begin to shift. Over time, there will be no more lying, no more conflict, no more war, and no more disease."

Charlie shook his head in total disbelief. "Are you pulling my leg?"

"No, I'm dead serious. This great shift began to be prophesied in the 1980s by many channels. Then, in the 1990s, and continued into the new millennium. The prophecy became very common. Channels such as Kryon, Kirael, Gaia, St. Germain, and many more have all heralded this great shift.

"At first, I was dubious about this so-called great shift. But then, as I read more of these channeled messages, I became a believer. These prophets convinced me because of the accuracy of their other prophecies of earth changes, economic, and social decline, which have all been accurate. I am now waiting diligently for this great shift, the final prophecy."

Charlie made a skeptical grimace. "Peace on Earth? Man, that doesn't seem possible."

"Well, it's not going to be peace on Earth overnight. Once the shift begins, it's going to take four generations complete. Social institutions will continue to deteriorate, earth changes will continue, and our spiritual beliefs will steadily transform. This coming shift will just increase the speed of the transformation. And, in the end, we will have a new civilization."

"More chaos, man," Billy said, shaking his head.

"Yes, it will look that way for a while," I said. "The prophecy is that less than a third of the global population will survive the shift."

"That is a lot of dead people," Billy said.

I nodded. "We can expect a lot more disease. On a positive note, after the shift begins, violence should begin to curtail. I wish I could say the same for earth changes. I don't expect them to decrease for at least another decade."

"What are you saying?" Charlie asked. "That things will get worse?"

"It looks like it in the near term," I said. "My guess is that peace on Earth will begin to manifest around 2035."

"I don't know if I can wait that long," Sam said, trying to get comfortable in his chair. "You know how hard it is to get food and electricity. We're barely getting by, man."

"I can try to help."

"How?" Charlie asked.

I looked into his eyes. "Life is not what it appears. You think you are your body, don't you? But you're not. Your body is nothing more than a suit, something that you wear temporarily.

"*We* are much more than we appear," I continued. "*Every one of us* is an advanced soul. No one is on this planet unless they are advanced. Everyone has earned a right to be here, to experience the shift. I know that I've lived more than a

Chapter Four – Kidnapped for Breakfast

thousand lives. It's probable that you have, too. Each of us is a unique soul. We're eternal, and we are much more than we perceive.

"If you like, I'll help you understand who you are and why you're here, if you're interested in finding out."

"Why would you do that?" Charlie asked in a surly, suspicious tone.

"Well, I live nearby and that's what I do. I teach spirituality. And I don't charge anything."

They all paused and looked at each other.

"Sounds good, man," Sam said, good naturedly, looking at his friends.

"Yeah, I like your karma," Billy added. "You know what you're talking about."

"All right," Charlie said, giving the final approval. "When do you want to come by?"

"How about once a week, for a couple of hours," I said. "How about Wednesday nights at 7 p.m.?"

Charlie nodded. "Yeah, we can do that."

We talked about meeting at the bus station, and then a young woman wandered into the room. She was pretty, thin, with long blonde hair and clear skin. She was barefoot, wearing pajamas and a T-shirt.

"Who's he?" she asked, cynically.

"A friend," Billy said. "Meet John."

"Sure," she replied, with obvious sarcasm. "When did you guys start making friends with people who shave? What's going on?" She stood with her arms crossed, tapping her foot, and waiting for answers. She was in her early twenties, with intense eyes and a lot of spunk. I instantly sensed that she was the leader of the house.

"Sis," Charlie said innocently, "I brought him to meet you. He's a New Age writer, just in from the Expo in Portland.

I thought you might want to talk to him. He was in the neighborhood."

"Did you guys force him to come here?" she asked, with a simmering glare.

"No," I interjected. "They asked me, and I said 'yes.'"

"Well, I don't believe you, but so be it." She walked over to the coffee pot and poured a cup. She brought the pot and several cups back with her.

"You look familiar," she said. "You're not John Randall, are you?"

"Yeah, I am. Have you read any of my books?"

"Whoa!" she said, surprised. "You *are* John Randall!"

"He's going to come over on Wednesday nights to talk with us," Charlie said. "He's going to teach us some of the things he knows."

This stunned the young woman. She looked at her brother and made a strange face. "This is too weird. John Randall is going to come to *our* house on Wednesday nights to teach *us*? And my brother Charlie is waiting in anticipation? I need more coffee…." She lifted her cup dramatically and took a deep sip.

"Nothing happens by accident," I said. "I ran into your brother, Billy, and Sam, for a reason. I'm beginning to believe that it was because of you. Obviously, you are the leader of the household. If you are the leader over men as strong as these, you must have a destiny to lead. I live nearby, and your energy drew me to you."

"This is heavy," she said, "and not something that I expected to happen. But perhaps you're right. So come back next Wednesday night, and we'll see how it goes."

I nodded and sensed that this was an opportunity to leave. "I need to get on my way. I have a long walk, and I've been traveling for many hours."

Chapter Four – Kidnapped for Breakfast

"Can't you stay for breakfast?" Billy asked.

"I'd really like to get going. Thanks, though. It was a pleasure meeting all of you."

"All right then," Charlie said. "We'll meet you at the bus station at 7 p.m. on Wednesday night."

"Okay, I'll be there," I said.

I was waiting for Charlie to threaten me if I didn't show up. But he knew that I knew he could find me. Now that he knew my name, I couldn't hide.

I rose, shook their hands, and went on my way. As I walked out, I wondered how I was going to explain this to Julie. Two hours later, I arrived home, just in time for breakfast.

Spirit Club

Chapter Five

Spirit Club Begins

When I rounded the corner of the park and saw our little community, I felt an overwhelming warmth in my heart. I actually felt good about the conditions in which we lived. We were getting by, and for the most part, we were content.

We had a good situation compared to the rest of the country. Shelter, food, water, electricity, and enough income to support us. We also used barter effectively. It wasn't unusual for us to trade the use of our truck for supplies, or materials to build another tent, or for other needs.

In many respects, we were extremely fortunate. We had everything we needed, and we had each other. The community was a large extended family. We shared, and we gave so much to each other that everyone felt like part of a family.

As I got closer, several people saw me and yelled my name. I smiled and waved, making my way to the eating area. Many people were having breakfast and talking. Kate ran to greet me. I picked her up and hugged her.

"Did you miss me?" I asked Kate.

She nodded. "I'm glad you're home."

I walked to Julie with Kate in my arms, then put her down and hugged and kissed Julie. She was sitting with our friends, so I joined them. We talked about my trip. The part about my interesting morning didn't come up for several minutes. Then someone asked how I got home from the bus station, and I told them about my little adventure.

Julie's eyes lit up. "What! Sometimes I don't know about you, John Randall. You are so stubborn!" she exclaimed. "Don't you know you have a wife and a child who *need* you? When are you going to learn?"

In a calm, assuring voice, I said, "Everything happens perfectly. If something happens to me, it's supposed to happen. So why worry? Why live in fear? Why not live with trust and joy in our hearts?"

That wasn't what Julie wanted to hear. She loved me, but she didn't always understand my spirituality.

"Why tempt fate?" she asked stubbornly.

I contemplated. "I follow my intuition, not logic. When I got off the bus, I felt like walking. And if I feel something, I usually follow through on it. If I don't live by feeling, I'll ignore the guidance of my soul."

"Oh … you make me so mad sometimes … you're so full of it!" she said in a loud voice. I could tell by her facial expression that she was extremely fearful and upset.

I started laughing. "You knew exactly what you got when you married me."

"Don't laugh," she replied angrily. "You're going to get yourself killed going downtown to teach those people."

"If that's my destiny…."

"Just like that? *That's* your answer?"

"Yes," I said calmly. "I told them I would teach them, and I will. Just like that."

"Don't be so smug. This is serious."

"So, we're having a fight?" I asked.

"Yes."

"You're sure?"

Chapter Five - Spirit Club Begins

"Yes."

"Hmm," I said. "I've been traveling for twenty-four hours, and you want me to think. Okay, let's have a short one. You go first."

Several people were listening at the next table and began laughing. It was common for Julie and me to have these strange fights. Everyone understood that we never took these skirmishes too seriously and that we were madly in love.

"I'm serious this time," she said. "I don't want you going down there at night."

"That's the best you can do?" I said. "Then this argument is going to be over very quickly. I'm on this planet to help people understand spirituality. That's why I'm here. Yes, I'm a husband and a father, but that's not why I'm here. I'm here to help people. When I see that I can, then I need to do it. If I don't, I will not achieve my contract." I squeezed her shoulders affectionately. "Julie, I *have* to follow my heart. You know that."

There was a long silence as she considered her reply.

"I'm sorry," she said, at last. "I guess it was the trip and you being away. I'm afraid that something will happen to you."

I raised my arms straight up in mock victory. Our friends seated across the table were laughing harder now.

I leaned over and kissed Julie affectionately. "I love you."

"I know," she said knowingly.

* * * * *

On Wednesday night, Julie took me downtown, resigned to the fact that I was going. We drove the Honda Accord, which was one of five vehicles that the community owned. On the drive, Julie relaxed behind the wheel. There was no more friction between us. "If this is what you feel you must do, John, then I'm not going to stand in your way."

I smiled. "Thank you."

Julie dropped me off at the bus station, where we had agreed to meet. I didn't have to look far to find Charlie, Billy, and Sam. They were waiting. We said our hellos and began walking to their house.

The walk was still another mile or so. The neighborhood where they lived was dark and dangerous, and I wasn't going to have someone drop me off at their house, or walk there alone at night. That's why I had them meet me at the bus station. It was close by, well-lit, and accessible.

I walked through the front door and was surprised to see a house full of people. There were at least twenty people in the living room and probably more in the kitchen. It was a festive atmosphere, with many people laughing and having a good time. I found Charlie's sister and introduced myself.

"Hi, I don't know your name?" I asked.

She smiled. "It's Kris. I'm really glad you came. I didn't think you would."

"This is what I do. I wanted to be here. Plus, I don't think your brother would have been happy if I was a no-show."

She laughed. "That's for sure. Are you ready to begin?"

"Yeah, I'm ready."

"Give me a few minutes to get everyone seated."

Kris went to work herding everyone into the living room. With her organizing abilities, it didn't take long. Even Charlie found a place in a short time. I was impressed.

Most of the room was occupied. People sat on couches, chairs, and on the floor. Kris pointed to a chair that faced the group and said it was for me. I sat in the designated chair and waited for everyone to quiet down. Then I introduced myself and began.

Chapter Five - Spirit Club Begins

"I write books and teach people about New Age spirituality. My focus is on the future and where we are headed as a civilization. One of my books is titled *New Thinking for the New Age*. I gave it this title because that's where we're headed: a new age. I write about and teach the spiritual principles that will be widely accepted in the emerging new age, or new civilization, whichever term you prefer.

"It's not hard to recognize that revolutionary events are happening today. It's also not hard to realize that we're not going back to the civilization that existed a few years ago. A new era is forming. A new civilization is emerging.

"Many of the ideas that I'm going to talk about tonight may be new to you, so I'll go slowly. Tonight is only an introduction. Over the next few weeks, I'll come back and share more. Gradually, I will share with you the spirituality of the future, that is, if you're still interested." I smiled, and most of them smiled back.

I wiggled in my chair, trying to get comfortable. "Tonight, I'm going teach you how to find your soul, and then I'll talk about duality: right and wrong, good and bad, and where those ideas come from.

"Okay, let's begin with your soul. We are not human, and these bodies are not us. We inhabit these bodies with our souls when we incarnate. This is not your first lifetime. Your soul has incarnated many times. I know this because only advanced souls are allowed to incarnate here. Nobody would choose Earth for their first lifetime.

"The soul is much more intelligent than our human brain. All of us have a dual intelligence, which comes from our brain and our soul. Have you ever wondered why some people are so talented at a young age, such as musicians or artists? That knowledge is not coming from their brain.

I scanned the room. "Has anyone had an NDE, a near-death experience?"

A lady in her thirties raised their hand.

"Excellent. When your soul popped out of your body, were you surprised that you had intelligence and that you could see and hear, even though you didn't have a body?"

"Yes," she said. "It was surreal. Our soul can see in all directions simultaneously and can hear sounds from almost any distance. The soul seemed to be almost limitless in its capability to see and hear. I had my NDE in the hospital. I popped out of my body, and I was hovering near the ceiling of my hospital room. I watched the doctors try to revive me."

"Thank you for sharing. After I am finished, you can tell everyone about your NDE. For now, I just want everyone to realize the soul is real and the soul is intelligent. I should add that it is also eternal. But more than anything else, the soul is always with us. It doesn't come and go. It's always here. It's what provides our consciousness. Our soul *is* our consciousness.

"Do you want to feel your soul?"

I scanned the audience.

"Sure," Kris said.

"Okay, everyone feel their hands using your consciousness. Feel them tingle. That is your soul. Notice that in order to feel your hands tingle, you have to quiet your mind. We'll get back to that in a moment.

"This is where you will have an epiphany. You think your identity is your ego-personality. But your soul consciousness is actually your true self, but you are not aware of it. When you feel your hands, there is an intelligence that's in the background. That consciousness that is feeling your hands is actually intelligent. And, here's the key, it's *not* your ego.

Chapter Five - Spirit Club Begins

Wrap your head around that. This is your other intelligence. It's your consciousness. It's your soul.

"The soul tries to guide us, but it is blocked by the ego. The ego is our personality-self, which is actually our fake-self. It isn't real. This is the personality-self that we create for this lifetime, but we don't take it with us when we die."

I looked at the lady who had the NDE. "Did you feel the ego, your false personality, when you had your NDE?"

Everyone in the room looked at her as she slowly shook her head no. "No, all that was left was my true self, which was pure love. I was much more than Earth-identity."

"Thank you," I said. "The ego-self does not care about our well-being. In fact, its job is to tempt you, distract you, and trap you from finding your soul. Its job is to keep you trapped in the illusion of this world. And the more you believe this world is real, the easier it is for the ego to control us. Once you find your soul, the ego loses its power controlling us, and we then can let the soul guide us.

"In essence, once we find our soul, we can tap into that intelligence and let it lead us. We can strip away the ego's grip on controlling us and push it aside. But we need to learn how to do this.

"And I'm going to teach how, right now. The ego is your chattering mind. The soul is only exposed when you quiet your mind and listen to it. You just did that when you felt your hands. Let me show you another way to quiet your mind. Let's say you are in a store, and a robber comes in with a gun. Your ego is going to make you feel afraid. What you need to do is relax, quiet your mind, and observe what is happening, without any thoughts. Just observe. Stand back using your mind, and observe. When you do that, your ego-mind shuts down, and the soul appears. The only thing that will be active is your consciousness, which is your soul.

"What you will be doing is creating space between your non-thinking ego-mind, which you have silenced, and your consciousness, which is your soul. Thus, you will tap into your soul and block the ego. You will block it from thinking. Remember, the ego can only exist in the chattering mind, which is your brain's memories. Your soul is more powerful than your ego because it is more intelligent. So, when we create this observational space, the ego is held at bay. And, walla, fear also goes away. Why? Because the soul does not know fear."

I paused to get the reaction from the room.

"Holy crap," Kris said. "That's some deep stuff, John."

I smiled. "In the future, everyone will know they have a soul and how to communicate with it. I just taught you how. Now you can practice. Learn how to quiet the mind by observing your thoughts, thereby exposing the soul and creating space between the ego and your consciousness. Make it a habit to say, 'Hi soul, how are you today.' And wait for an answer. Begin talking to your soul. Form a relationship with your soul. I talk to mine every single day, and so should you.

"More than anything else, stop letting your ego direct your life. Instead, let your soul direct it."

"How do we do that?" Kris asked.

"First, you need to know the difference between the ego and the soul, and it's pretty easy to know the difference. The core of the soul is love, and it only cares about love. So, what does love have in common? Only one thing: virtue. All virtues are synonymous with love. These would be kindness, friendliness, compassion, unconditional love, generosity, service, helpfulness, humanity, et cetera. These are the only things the soul cares about. So, if your chattering mind wants you to do something that is contrary to virtue, that is the ego. When that happens, you simply quiet the mind and ask the

Chapter Five – Spirit Club Begins

soul what to do. This takes practice, but it's possible for all of you.

"My favorite quote of all time is from Mary Magdalene in her gospel. She says, 'I go now to the silence.' She is talking about listening to her soul. We can all do this to get direction. The soul's guidance is true. The soul knows what we need.

"Now, you may think this is all BS, but I'm telling you the truth. The soul is real, and you can connect to it. You can also have a relationship with it. But understand that the soul *only* cares about love and virtue. It will do everything it can to guide you to love. Conversely, the ego will do everything it can to stop you from finding the soul.

"The movie *Star Wars* was about good and evil. It showed that humanity was in a struggle of good versus evil. This is false. The truth is that each individual is in a struggle of exposing their false ego, and trying to find their soul, or true self, which is love. This is the truth that will set you free."

I paused. "We don't have all night, so I can't take questions. I'm sure you have several, but I want to move on to the next topic, which is duality. Is there such a thing as right and wrong?"

I waited for an answer. Many were stunned that I had actually posed the question.

A lady next to Kris said, "Of course there is." She was wearing all black and sitting in a chair directly in front of me. Her eyes were intense, and her demeanor was serious.

"You're sure?" I asked. "You can prove this?"

She hesitated. "No. I can't prove it. It's a feeling."

I smiled. "Thank you. Yes, it is a feeling. Life is about feelings, not logic. Logically, there is no such thing as right or wrong. One person's opinion of wrong is another person's only course of action. Each of us has choices about what we think is right or wrong. Each of us decides by our personal perceptions or feelings. We make our choices because we *feel* them. Logic, or truth, has nothing to do with it.

"From our soul's standpoint, there is no such thing as right or wrong. All of our choices are the right choices for that moment. The choices we make are made because we feel that they are right. In fact, everyone chooses what they think is best for them at any particular moment. Thus, no matter what choice we ultimately make, it *is* the right choice for us, individually."

"Wait a minute," the same lady said. "You're implying that there is no standard of morality."

I nodded. "Black is white, and white is black. Everything we've been told about life we can throw out the window. Indeed, there is no such thing as morality."

"Whoa," Sam said from the back of the room. "You're pretty deep, man."

"We can have personal morals," I said, "but we can't assign morality to someone else. Thus, there is no such thing as universal morals. You can't assign my morals, and I can't assign yours. Indeed, all choices are valid, and all experiences are valid." I paused.

"I can't accept that," said the lady. "You're saying that it's okay for people to harm other people, even children."

"I'm not encouraging that. I'm just sharing knowledge to which I have been exposed. Could the sources be wrong? It's possible. It could be misinformation and that I am wrong. Thus, you have to decide for yourself what you believe. *You* have to determine your own beliefs. But when you judge another as morally wrong, you are not seeing the complete picture."

I scanned the room and then continued. "I do know that nothing can happen to anyone unless they want it to happen.

Chapter Five - Spirit Club Begins

We create our own experiences, and nothing happens to us by accident."

"How do you know that?" she asked, in a challenging tone, which implied that I had to be wrong.

"I can't prove it, if that's what you want to know. We each have to learn this for ourselves. But this will be widely known in the future. I can, however, give supporting arguments. People do so-called immoral acts *because* of society. It's never just one person's fault. To blame only a perpetrator is naïve. Furthermore, victims always agree on a soul level to endure negative experiences. There are no random victims. Life is much more complex than we perceive."

I looked back at the thirty-year-old woman. "The very act of defining morality creates immorality. To define morality for other people requires judgment, leading people to be judged in a moral way. This judgment actually creates the behavior that you are trying to prevent. For instance, hate creates more hate, condemnation creates more condemnation, war creates more war. Let me explain."

I paused and scanned the room. The audience was attentive and receptive. I was relaxed and felt comfortable, which was odd, considering the neighborhood. "When you judge someone, you are inflicting emotional pain on them, because deep inside that person knows they do not deserve your judgment. This emotional trauma will then often manifest in a so-called immoral way. Thus, the people who defined morality actually created the energy that led to the act they forbade.

"By defining morality for others, we claim that God approves of this judgment. We claim that we know what God wants and what God perceives as right or wrong. Furthermore, we claim that we have the right to condemn others.

"*The Scarlet Letter* by Nathaniel Hawthorne is a good example of a community deciding the fate of others, using a code of morality. In this book, a married woman, whose husband is lost at sea, gets pregnant and must wear an 'A' for adulteress. Did God really condemn her behavior? Does the creator of the universe judge our choices? Were we created so that we could be judged for our moral failings? To this day, we still use such a system. But soon, we will see the fallacy of such a system.

"Duality," I continued, "which is the belief in right and wrong, creates judgment. From judgment comes emotional pain, and from pain comes the manifestation of what we call evil. Duality creates a civilization imbued with emotional pain, and no one can escape the impact. In other words, we have evil because we have created evil. If we want evil to go away, then we have to stop judging each other. The world has been living in emotional pain for thousands of years. But, rest assured, that is about to end." I paused.

"How soon, John?" Kris asked in a calm tone.

"Very soon. We will get to see the nascent beginning of this trend. Love will soon begin to flourish across the planet, and the trend toward peace on Earth will have begun. As love becomes more and more prevalent, life will steadily get better. We are the progenitors. We are here to usher in the New Age. And it is happening *now*. People are beginning to realize that duality is an illusion, and that indeed there is no reason to judge anyone's behavior.

"I haven't told you why yet, and now I will. Our soul is consciousness, but what is the source of that consciousness? Are we self-contained? The answer is no. For, if we were self-contained, then telepathy would be impossible. Consciousness is not only not self-contained, but it is interrelated. In fact, there is only one consciousness, which we all share. This

Chapter Five - Spirit Club Begins

single consciousness is also called the law of one. That single consciousness is the Creator, or God, which term you prefer.

"And guess what? Since there is only one consciousness, that means that we are God. Well, we are aspects of God. We are individuations of God. We are all eternal, and we are equal. God has no favorites."

"Holy crap," Sam said. "That can't be right."

I smiled at Sam. "It is right. It is true. What is true is always true. As this truth is revealed, instead of judging each other, we will begin to love each other. Judgment and morality will wane."

"Society needs some code of conduct," said the lady from the front row in black, still doubting my words.

"Yes, that's true. However, in the future, this will be done more on an individual level than a societal level. Each individual will have their own code of morality. Each individual is responsible for their own behavior. We each know what is right and wrong for ourselves. Our behavior dictates how those around us respond. If we want to have friends, jobs, or relationships with others, then we better act accordingly. My point is that it is impossible to determine or dictate someone else's morality. They have to figure it out for themselves, and if they get it wrong, we should be empathetic more so than judgmental. That is how God thinks."

A man near the back of the room raised his hand. I pointed to him. "Can you stand up?" I asked. "I can't see you very well." My view of him was obscured in the crowded room.

He stood. He was in his sixties, with greased-back, short dark hair. There was an aura of intelligence in his eyes and demeanor. He cleared his throat. "What about children? Should we teach them what we think is right and wrong?"

"Your example should be enough," I said. "Let them figure it out. Let them determine their own personal moral codes. They're going to, anyway." Everyone laughed. "The more you push your moral codes on your kids, the more you will either push them away from you, or the more you will confuse them. I say this because the world is entering a new era where right and wrong are meaningless.

"What is true is always true, and the future is all about truth, objective truth. There is no objective truth with morality, because there is not right and wrong. Everything is perfection.

"Since you brought up children," I said, "let's talk about them. From birth, children are judged as lacking knowledge, and they are perceived as naïve. Instead of being loved, they are judged. Instead of being respected and honored as evolved souls, which they are, they are judged as being irresponsible and ill-prepared. The message they receive from us is, 'Prove to us adults that you're worthy.' And when they fail to live up to our expectations, we judge them as lacking. Even worse, as losers. We imbue emotional pain on them when they don't deserve it.

"What are the ramifications of our judgment? What do we push them to do? In a word, experience. And the more painful the judgment, the more intense the experiences they choose, often experiences that are considered immoral. Instead of trying to teach children right from wrong, we need only honor and love them. For our children to develop into mature adults, the best thing we can give them is confidence in themselves, and not tell them how to live their lives, or what is acceptable and what isn't. Again, teach by example.

"People do so-called immoral acts, not because they weren't taught right from wrong, or given stern discipline as children. Such experiences result from a lack of love in a world where everyone is quick to judge. Like I said, today we live in

Chapter Five – Spirit Club Begins

a society filled with emotional pain rather than love. And it takes a lot of pain for two high school boys to bring guns to school and murder twelve of their fellow students, like what happened at Columbine High School in Littleton, Colorado. Of course, that was only one of hundreds of mass shootings in recent years."

I paused, as we reminisced about that omen in 1999 that foretold things to come. "It's not that difficult to be a parent. All we have to do is love our children; give them self-confidence; let them do what they want; and be there for them when they need us. Trust me, if Hitler would have had more love as a child, he would not have become a monster."

"I don't know about letting children or teenagers do what they want," said a middle-aged lady sitting on the floor in front, only a few feet away. "My son would play video games all day long."

I looked at her. "Well, there's nothing wrong with deciding for them what you think is acceptable. You can raise your children any way you want. But there will be ramifications. Ideally, children at a young age should be allowed to learn to guide themselves. This is how we give our children self-confidence. We show them that we believe in them. The minute we begin telling them how to live their lives, is the minute they start depending on us. If we want powerful children, we must empower them.

"I have a seven-year-old daughter named Kate. I'm trying to teach her to make her own decisions. At this age, she still wants to be babied. She wants us to pay constant attention to her. But if I do what she wants, I'll take away her power. Yes, I have to guide her to a certain extent. If I see her doing something that I think could cause a problem, I do tell her. But I'm trying to let Kate create her own life. I'm trying to allow her to create it. At her age, giving her the freedom to do what she wants isn't an easy thing for me to do." Several people laughed.

"She still wants me and my wife, Julie, to create her life for her. Emotionally, she's very manipulative. Usually, it's difficult to get her to understand that *she* is in control of her own life. I treat Kate as an equal, as a person. And I know she's an advanced soul. I know she's capable. My responsibility is to allow Kate to use her own capabilities, and not for me to do things for her."

"It sounds like you honor and respect your daughter without her having to prove her worthiness to you. Is that what you're implying?" Kris asked.

I nodded. "Yes, that's where love begins. You nurture it, and it grows and expands. Okay, we need to get back to the main topic: duality. So, there's no such thing as universal right or wrong. Right and wrong are defined by each of us individually, as our own personal codes. Thus, our opinions of right and wrong are just opinions.

"If we want to experience something that we feel is wrong, we can. We each have the right to follow our feelings. And the outcomes of these experiences are valid. Experiences are not judged by God as right or wrong. God's love is unconditional. God allows us to experience whatever we choose.

"Let me tell you a story. This man has just overdosed on heroin. He has left his body and is staring down at it in awe. Then he becomes concerned, because he realizes that he has died and passed into a new reality and that his previous life had ramifications. He didn't know that his soul was real, and now he knew that it was. He becomes nervous and worried because he had done many so-called immoral and bad things. He had raped. He had murdered. He had stolen. He had lied and cheated. He had treated friends and people in ways that made him recoil with guilt. Now, floating above his body, he

Chapter Five – Spirit Club Begins

wonders what the ramifications of his actions would be. He thought that, if anyone was destined for hell, it was him.

"Then he noticed an angel, or what he perceived to be an angel, flying toward him. Suddenly, he felt calm. It was the first time in years that he felt sober and had a clear mind. Instead of feeling guilty, he felt an incredible feeling of bliss. He waited for the angel and felt no reason to run.

"The angel smiled, and love radiates from her aura. The man waited for the angel to speak. 'I have come for you,' the angel says telepathically. 'Are you ready?'

"The man asked if they were going to Heaven. The angel nods and says telepathically, 'That was a hard life for you. Let's go see if you can have an easier one next time.' And they fly to heaven."

I scanned the room. "What is the moral of the story?"

Kris smiled at me. "That God loves everyone equally."

"Good answer." I smiled back.

I looked at my watch. "Sorry folks. I'm out of time." I stood. "Next week, same time. I'll see all of you then. Thanks for coming. Next time, I'll try to answer some of your questions."

I walked around the room and shook hands and hugged a few people. The people were friendly and enjoyed the opportunity to think about new ideas. I had the feeling that most would be back next week.

Charlie, Sam, Billy, and I were out the door and headed for the bus station. I really appreciated their company. I didn't want to walk alone to the bus station at night.

* * * * *

The next week, I spent all of my time working at the restaurant and helping my community. My life usually was busy because there were always things to do. Jed, our community leader, always found something for me to do when I had free time.

Jed was a Capricorn. His natal chart had the sun in Capricorn, Capricorn rising, moon in Aries, and Mercury in Taurus. He was always marching around and telling us what to do. If he found out that I was available, he put me to work.

Everyone in our small community had a role, or roles, to assume. One of my roles was to go to Bakersfield three times a year and pick up a load of food. I also was the resident spiritual teacher and a helper. Jed made sure that my role of helper was constantly honored. He even came by our tent to get my work schedule at the restaurant.

One of my roles was gardening in the community garden and greenhouse. I actually liked it, even though it was hard work. The garden was pretty big. It consumed nearly an acre of the park. We had become squatters when the park was abandoned by the city. We also had a large greenhouse.

We grew all kinds of vegetables and had several fruit trees. The climate had changed in the last few years, with the northern latitudes much colder, and our hot weather much milder in the summer. We found that we could grow just about anything.

Sonya was the full-time gardener; it was her garden. Jed told me that I was needed in the garden at least once a week. I reported to Sonya, and she put me to work. I usually carried pails of water to hand-water the plants because we had only a few short hoses. I also planted, weeded, and harvested.

On many occasions, I brought Kate with me. And, as we worked together, we talked. Sometimes she got bored and found other people to work with. I enjoyed watching her interact with the other members of the community.

Jed also used my abilities to acquire necessities. He told me what was needed and then expected me to obtain

Chapter Five - Spirit Club Begins

it. Sometimes he gave me a list. Other times, he just told me where to go. One time, I went to Phoenix to find a part for a broken refrigerator. Jed told me that a friend of his had the part, and I was to go and get it. Since then, I've never been surprised by Jed's requests. I just do as I'm told.

Other people in the community also had roles, such as a handyman. Several of the men could fix just about anything, such as plumbing, electrical, cement, and so on. Some people made things. We had a woodworker who could make any kind of furniture, an artist who painted beautiful designs onto the furniture, and several women who made clothes. These were only a few of the roles that people assumed.

Julie was the community school teacher. She taught the children who were less than sixteen years of age. Currently, she had ten students. Once students turned sixteen, they took courses online, using the Internet. If they excelled, they could apply to the University of Arizona to get a degree online, which was free.

The public school system still existed, but the condition of society was so dire that many children left the school system. Most of the parents in our tiny community didn't even consider sending their children to public schools. What was the point? What were they going to be taught that Julie couldn't teach them? And we preferred to have the children with us at all times because the city had become so dangerous.

* * * * *

I went back downtown for our weekly discussion group the following Wednesday. Charlie, Sam, and Billy were waiting when Julie dropped me off at the bus station. The four of us walked the few blocks to their house.

They told me that they had lived together at their current address since 2027. Employment had been difficult for them to find in the last few years. Most of the work they found was temporary, and often only for a few days. They were constantly broke, and food was difficult to obtain.

I walked into the house and was surprised to see that there were even more people than last week. I said hello to several people I recognized from before. I made a point of walking over to Kris and saying hello. Somehow, I felt that she was one of the main reasons I was there.

She had already organized the room, and I had the feeling that everyone knew where they were supposed to sit. Once we got started, there wouldn't be any floor space available at all. I decided that we'd better begin before anyone got claustrophobic.

"Kris? Are we ready?"

She didn't miss a beat. She started pointing and giving orders and, in less than two minutes, everyone was seated. Her leadership abilities were impressive.

"Last week," I said as I began, "I introduced some New Age concepts. I talked about finding your soul and the duality of right and wrong, and how this duality is personal and not universal. I was sharing spiritual truth, and because you came back, I think you are ready to explore more spiritual truth. Tonight, I'm going to talk about the spiritual path, and how spirituality can lead us to the ultimate truth, to enlightenment.

"Enlightenment is the awareness that we are God; or, if you prefer, an aspect of God. Of course, no one *is* God. We are part of God, but by being a part of God, our potential becomes unlimited. Not the potential of us as humans, but the potential of our soul to evolve.

"Most of you do not know this, but the reason you are alive, the reason you are on this planet, is to remember that you are God. Life is about remembering, and each of us is

Chapter Five - Spirit Club Begins

pursuing enlightenment in our own way. Everyone is steadily becoming more spiritually aware, even if they don't realize it.

"This is what our experiences are for, be they negative or positive. It is important to understand that all experiences are valid, and that nothing is wasted. We are always learning, and always becoming more aware that we are God."

Kris raised her hand, and I pointed at her. "Do you mean that we will each personally become aware that we are God?"

I nodded. "Yes, that is our destiny. Maybe not in this lifetime, but eventually. Many old souls on this planet are getting close to this awareness. That is what my talk is about tonight."

I paused and maneuvered my chair, getting more comfortable. "The ego, or what we perceive our identities to be, is an illusion. We talked about this last week. The ego is nothing more than a temporary personality." I pointed to my head. "The ego is up here in the brain, in our memories since birth. The ego is fragile, mercurial, and constantly changing because it is something we are constantly creating. In fact, our chattering mind is literally our ego, which is continually trying to define itself."

I smiled and scanned the room. Everyone was in rapt attention.

"The ego tricks us into thinking that God can be found only in our mind, by using our thoughts. When I use the term mind, I'm referring to our brain - our memories. However, God cannot be found there. God can only be found with our feelings. You have to feel God's presence to know that God exists."

I scanned all the skeptical faces. "Then where do we find God?" I pointed at my heart. "The heart. The heart is the gateway to God. It is the source of our wisdom. God communicates to us by feeling. And what you feel in your heart applies only to yourself, which is why spirituality is a personal experience.

"This is why meditation is so important to the religions of the East, which have produced most of the great avatars. Jesus was an Essene, and they were known for meditation. Christianity should have had a foundation of meditation all along, but it was lost when the Gnostics were burned at the stake.

"Meditation quiets our chattering mind and gets us in tune with our hearts and puts us in contact with our higher selves and our spirit guides. The path to God is through the heart. It's a path of spiritual awareness and an expansion of awareness. This is the path of many people on the planet today who are coming to know themselves as one with God."

I paused. "Now, most of you have not yet found this path. Why? The ego. The ego rebels against the heart and smothers it with mindless chatter. The ego has convinced you that the heart pathway does not exist. However, once you open this pathway, your life will never be the same.

"The ego obscures the heart by focusing on its false identity. This ego identity is constantly chattering in your mind and convincing you that it is real. In fact, the ego's primary mission is to reinforce this identity. It is constantly playing a game of what I call identity building. The ego is always striving to either maintain its identity or expand it. Thus, the ego gets you trapped in the illusion of the external world, always chasing after happiness, security, or both. Both of which are illusions.

"Whereas the heart will lead us down a path of love and relationship with our true self, the ego will try to control us using fear, temptation, or societal influences. The ego will try to convince us of what behavior is acceptable, and thereby will control our path. For instance, the path of a Catholic or a

Chapter Five - Spirit Club Begins

Christian Protestant has little chance for evolving spiritually because those paths are confined to the ego."

I scanned the room to see who was paying attention. "Let me make a statement here. All beliefs are valid. In other words, as far as God is concerned, there is no right or wrong belief. From our beliefs, we have experiences. If you limit your beliefs to exclude the heart as the conduit to God, then you will limit your spiritual path." I paused.

Kris raised her hand, and I pointed at her. "Is it really that simple? If I open my heart to God, then I will become more spiritually aware?"

I shook my head. "Not necessarily, because the ego is a very capable foe. To open the heart, you will also have to quiet the mind and marginalize the ego. This is where meditation helps. Once you quiet the false ego, which is the chattering mind, and listen with the heart, then you will become more spiritual. That is the secret that has been withheld from humanity."

I paused, and the room was totally silent. I could feel the tangible excitement in the room, as many were experiencing a sudden epiphany.

A lady in front asked a question. "So, you're saying that God doesn't care about my past, only my future? God is waiting patiently for me to discard my ego and open my heart?"

I nodded. "Yes. Yes. Beautifully said! What is your name?"

"Mary."

I smiled, and slowly continued. "The Goddess energy. How appropriate. All of your past experiences were worth experiencing. All experiences lead to the ultimate goal, which is enlightenment." I grinned. "God doesn't judge. Do you know why? Because *we* are God. Everyone in this room is an expression of God. In fact, there is no separation between us and God. Separation is a lie.

"Before you discount this, think about it. Why couldn't it be true? Couldn't God, the creator, create a world to experience life as if anew? Couldn't God create aspects of itself, where the aspects – us – experience life as if anew? Most surely, this is a possibility. In fact, it has already been proven by quantum physics that everything is connected. The ultimate reality is unity, oneness." I paused.

The tall, sixty-year-old gentleman with the slicked-back dark hair was closer tonight, only a few feet away. He cleared his throat. "So, you're saying that life is an illusion? That we're all imagining being separate from each other?"

"Yes, but even though life is an illusion, it is also very real. For instance, every thought that we have impacts our lives and the lives of others. Our thoughts impact the lessons that our souls are learning. Thus, every thought has impact. Think about it? That's pretty *real*. When we begin to perceive the reality of life, it's quite fascinating. The mystery of life is that it is an illusion and real at the same time. What is real is our soul, which is eternal, and is learning new lessons every day. What is illusion is everything else, such as our bodies, this room, and the entire planet.

"To understand how life works," I continued, "we have to perceive the pervasive consciousness that interlinks everything, which is the unity of life. Some call this the law of one. Others call it oneness or All That Is. That consciousness is God. In other words, God is All That Is. Nothing ... nothing is separate from God. Many quantum scientists have already realized this, and in the near future, it will be a proven fact."

I paused. "Did that sink in?"

Several people smiled.

Chapter Five - Spirit Club Begins

"We are all *one*," I said. "There is no separation between anyone or anything. We are God. We are eternal. We are divine. And there is nothing that any of us needs to do in order to maintain our divinity. There is no salvation. There is no saving a soul. No one needs to be saved. God doesn't need help. In fact, what we perceive ourselves to be, our ego, is not who we really are. What we are experiencing on this planet is only a fragment of our true selves. Most of you in this room have lived thousands of lives, and your souls are highly evolved. There are spiritual masters in this room, and we don't even know who you are.

"Let me make another statement. You have nothing to achieve in this life except your contract. This contract is the agreement you made with your higher self before you incarnated, which your spirit guides are helping you to achieve. Our contract always has to do with our soul development. They are never about materialistic gain, or even improving civilization. They usually have to do with something such as controlling our selfishness, living without fear, or asserting ourselves with courage.

"We think that we need to achieve things, but this is generally not true. Of course, if your karma dictates that you achieve, then there's nothing wrong with achieving. But if you don't feel compelled to achieve, it's okay not to. Instead, follow your heart, follow your passion. Do what you feel compelled to do. This is how we are heart led.

"Everyone is growing spiritually. No matter what we do in this life, we will evolve. Spiritual growth is inevitable, even if we are caught up in our egos. We do, however, have a choice. We can choose to open our hearts and speed up the spiritual process. That's one of the reasons why I teach. Expanding our spiritual consciousness is a very real choice in life."

I rubbed the back of my neck and stretched my neck. "Each of us is climbing a spiritual ladder. We're climbing upward, as our souls evolve. But, know that spiritual evolution is natural and inevitable. There is no timetable.

"My goal is to help people become more spiritually aware. I like to help people climb the ladder of spiritual awareness and become more conscious. I'm helping others to evolve more rapidly. However, what I teach isn't for everyone, because not everyone is on the fast track and wants to get to know their higher self."

I paused. "Okay, let's speed up your evolution. Let's talk more about these spiritual truths. Life isn't about *being* good. It's about *being*. Life isn't about achieving. It's about *being*. Life isn't about doing. It's about *being*.

"Just about everyone in this room doesn't understand what I just said." They laughed. "However, before I leave tonight, I'm going to try to help you understand."

I smiled. "Life is about being. You do this by embracing today and ignoring the future. If you're thinking about the future, then your ego is in control. That's how we lived in the past. Now, you need to embrace your experiences and remain in the present. Whatever befalls you during your day, embrace it. Accept every moment as *your* creation. Accept your experiences as something that you need. Just go with it and see where it leads. Try to live day to day, instead of constantly thinking about the future.

"Try to be in the present moment. Then, when someone asks how you are doing, you can say, 'I'm not doing, I'm being.'

"There is really only one way not to think about the future, and that is trust. You have to start trusting God, trusting that your life is going to be perfect. Only then can you live day-to-day and experience *being*. However, trust comes

Chapter Five - Spirit Club Begins

second. Before you can trust God, you have to love your self. That's the starting point." I paused.

A middle-aged man, seated on the floor only a few feet from me, asked, "How do we learn to love ourselves?"

"Spiritual awareness," I replied. "Bartholomew, a channeled spirit that I've read, says that everyone is suffering from a broken heart. He means that our separation from each other, and our separation from God, have left an emptiness in our hearts. I agree. This is why self-love is so difficult.

"People judge themselves as lacking or unworthy. This self-judgment is actually a denial of self. We deny who we are, which is God, and we deny our divinity. Each of us is divine, but we don't act that way, and we don't feel that way about ourselves. Can you see how this belief has created the world in which we live? Can you see how a change in this belief will create a new world?

"If you can become spiritually aware that indeed you are divine, then self-love becomes very natural. The steps are as follows. First, you find your soul. Second, you begin to have a relationship with your soul. Third, you become aware that your soul is God and so are you."

A hand went up in the back of the room. I pointed to a teenage girl. She had long, curly brown hair and brown eyes. "I want to change and find my soul, and I see others in this room who want to change as well, but what about the soldiers and the government? They don't seem to care about the changes you're talking about."

"Thank you for the question," I said. "Those of the old energy are powerless; they just don't know it yet. Ignore them. Focus on you and focus your attention on the new energy. In time, the soldiers will disband. Treat them as irrelevant and you will hasten their demise. Don't engage with them. Ignore them. They are the past and won't be part of the future."

I grinned. "We're approaching a new world. Every day, more people are learning that they are divine, and that we are one. Once this belief is held, it leads to other new beliefs. People are beginning to accept themselves as divine, and self-love is flourishing.

"This is happening *now*," I continued. "The planet is transforming as we speak. New beliefs and a new spirituality are rising. Love is beginning to flow. Can you feel it? Can you feel the harmony in this room, just from us talking about the new spirituality?

"I have been more content these last few years than ever before in my life. It seems as if the deeper society falls, the more content I become. I can sense that we are headed to a good place, a place filled with harmony and joy, a place where people will love each other. The emotional pain of the past is about to end. No longer will we need to read the paper with trepidation about the misfortunes of others."

I leaned forward. "Do you want to help in this transition? Then, the best thing that you can do is to be yourself. Just *be*. Live day to day with self-love. Don't care about tomorrow. Just live today in the present moment and be present. When you are in harmony, you create harmony for others. When you love yourself, you will love others, and they will spread love. In other words, your love will rub off on others. It's like a chain reaction.

"In fact, this is called the frequency of love. You can achieve it as follows. First, be present. Second, embrace uncertainty and accept everything that happens as either a blessing or a lesson. Third, always be neutral, embracing unconditional love. In other words, don't react with judgment. If you follow these three steps, you will carry the frequency of love wherever you go. And spread it around like fairy dust.

Chapter Five - Spirit Club Begins

"There's another thing that Bartholomew says. He says to take off your head and put it under your arm. In other words, when your ego tries to get your attention, but you know it isn't important, ignore it. Most things aren't worth thinking about, except actions that you need to make in the present moment.

"The ego wants you to constantly think about the future, or to constantly judge right and wrong. Tell your ego to shut up. Take your head off, and put it under your arm. Literally imagine your head under your arm. If you do that, your mind will shut off. It's a fun little trick to control the ego for a few moments.

"Another trick I like to use, is to place my consciousness outside of my body and then look back at myself. If you do this, your chattering mind will be silenced. There are a lot of different ways to silence your chattering mind. Try to find something that works for you."

I paused and scanned the room. "Every problem that exists today arose from the belief that we are not divine. Once this belief is changed, the world will change...."

"So," Kris interrupted, "you're saying that we need to recognize ourselves and everyone else as God, as divine beings?"

I became animated. "Exactly. That's where we have to get to. We have to see God everywhere we look. How powerful do you think you are? What if I told you that not one event has happened in your life that you did not create? *That* is how powerful you are. Remember when Jesus said that we can do everything he did and more? That's *how* powerful we are. Do you see the ramifications of our denial of our divinity? Our focus on ego has thrown *everything* out of balance. Our egos have created a hell on earth.

"We need to undo all of the beliefs that have created the mess we have today. We have to awaken. And guess what?

We're going, too. We get to be the generation that awakens. We should feel very fortunate to have a front row seat."

I looked down at my watch and rose. "That's all the time I have tonight. Thanks for coming. I'm sorry I don't have time to answer more questions. Next week, though, I'll answer all of your questions. And bring your friends. We'll squeeze them in a corner somewhere." Several people laughed.

I shook a few hands and answered some easy questions before leaving with Charlie, Sam, and Billy.

Chapter Six

The Spirit Club Grows

On Friday, my community awoke to a power outage. This was nothing new. Sometimes the power stayed off for days. The power company wasn't as dependable as in the past. Now, when something broke or needed to be fixed, the power company would not (or could not) fix it in a matter of hours.

Our backup energy sources were solar and propane. Two dozen solar panels fed batteries that generated power for the park. We turned them on only during outages. And they provided enough electricity for tents and the kitchen.

We also had a couple of thousand-gallon tanks of propane. Those were mainly used for hot showers when our natural gas was out, although occasionally we used them for cooking. Generally, one tank always had a plentiful supply. We used propane only as a backup source, so it didn't cost a lot of money to maintain.

These power outages usually occurred once or twice a month, but they rarely lasted more than a day or two.

The biggest problem wasn't energy, but clean water. We usually always had water, but it wasn't always usable. The garden was never threatened with drought, but we were constantly searching for clean water for cooking or showers.

The problem was the water treatment plants. A lot of the water we received was recycled and had to be treated. The treatment plants in Tucson were constantly breaking down, and the untreated water was dreadful.

It was easy to know when the treatment plants weren't working. Our water would turn brown and had a strong odor. Even if we boiled and filtered it, the water was polluted. So, we couldn't use it for cooking, and bathing became problematic. Most of us did not take showers when the water was untreated. The stench alone was nauseating, let alone the risk of cleaning oneself with contaminated water.

We had a five-thousand-gallon water tank that we filled when the treatment plants were working. But five thousand gallons didn't last long. And when the treatment plants broke down for weeks at a time, our tank would run dry in a few days. When we ran out of water, we either went to wells near the Colorado River, or sometimes made trips to California. Finding clean water was, by far, the biggest headache that we had to endure.

We had at least fifty water bottles, each holding five gallons. We would throw about half of these bottles in the back of the big truck and set out to find a source. Sometimes it was easy to find. For instance, we knew several farmers nearby who would sell water from their wells at a cheap price. And sometimes when the treatment plants were down, the water district gave away clean water from a nearby well.

Unfortunately, there were very few private wells, which were owned by farmers or large estates. To drill a new well meant a huge amount of money because water rights were exorbitant. Water is life, and when water is scarce, it becomes a valuable commodity. We didn't have, nor would we likely ever obtain, our own well. We all realized this and simply accepted our fate.

There was one bright side to the water problem: the weather had changed in the last few years. No longer was the

Chapter Six - The Spirit Club Grows

average temperature in triple digits during the summer, and rainfall was increasing dramatically. If the weather continued like this, water would be plentiful soon. The water table would continue to rise, and reservoirs would certainly fill.

*****

On the following Wednesday night, I went back downtown to the bus station. As usual, Charlie, Sam, and Billy were waiting to greet me. I now found myself recognizing various things, and the landscape was becoming more familiar.

On this night, my mind took in my surroundings, and I wondered how things used to be. I looked at tattered billboards and wondered when they had held their last advertisement. I looked at empty businesses and wondered when they had met their demise. I glanced here and there, and my mind processed all of the data. This area had once been vibrant, and not that long ago.

Charlie, Sam, Billy, and I weren't talking. In fact, they usually were quiet, keeping a vigilant eye on the neighborhood. Tonight, I had a chance to relax and analyze the scenery. I knew this would be one of my few visits downtown at night, so I tried to get the most out of the experience.

An abandoned grocery store caught my eye. The first two times I had walked past it, I had only glanced in its direction. But tonight, I made an attempt to see what was going on inside. It was apparent that many people lived there.

The number of homeless people in Tucson was astounding. The fair weather and the ability to obtain food made Tucson a haven for people in southern Arizona. The streets teemed with them. I couldn't count them all. In the few short blocks that we walked from the bus station, I saw over a thousand homeless people. They were everywhere.

As I walked by the homeless on this night, I allowed them the respect they deserved. I knew that many were just as spiritually advanced as me. I knew they were suffering hardship. I knew their emotional pain was intense. Thus, I did not stare at them and inflict more pain. Instead, I looked at the buildings and the decaying infrastructure. I looked at the lights and the pavement ahead of me, anything that would distract me from staring.

I wondered how much more decay this area could take before people began to leave. It was stunning how far Tucson had fallen in a short period of time. Before society began to fall, I had wondered how this great nation would collapse. I knew that the economy would deteriorate rapidly, but I still wondered how it would happen. We were so wealthy, and our standard of living was so high. It seemed nearly impossible to me that this nation could fall, yet I believed it to be true.

Nearly all of those who I tried to tell thought I had come to the wrong conclusion. I understood their misgivings and skepticism. America was such a strong nation. Our infrastructure at one time was the best in the world. Our multi-trillion-dollar economy was incredibly dynamic: healthcare, farming, manufacturing, finance, technology, telecommunications, chemicals, pharmaceuticals, and entertainment. That is only a short list of the trillion-dollar industries that existed. Add to that, seventy-plus years of prosperous growth since 1945. At the beginning of 2020, people were in no mood to even consider the imminent demise of the U.S.A.

I remember thinking that it was the perfect time for a fall because nobody expected it. People would be so shocked by the sudden turn of events that they wouldn't be prepared. Chaos would ensue, and fear and panic would be rampant. Our economic system would implode from debt, and people

Chapter Six – The Spirit Club Grows

would lose faith in the future. The underpinning of the economy and confidence in the future would be shattered.

I knew that it was coming, but the sheer improbability kept everyone else hypnotized and oblivious to our fate. This great nation would fall in a very short period of time, and few were prepared. I had known this as early as 1989 and had tried to tell people, but it was of no use. Unless they had the ability to believe it, they weren't going to.

As I walked the streets that night on my way to the meeting, I thought back about how the economic collapse had come about and how fast it had actually occurred.

The first sign had been the financial crisis and stock market crash. That led to high unemployment and a plethora of housing foreclosures. Then came a global economic malaise, leading to the implosion of the global financial system. Boom, boom, boom. Just like that, and it was done.

*****

The approach to their neighborhood was especially dark that night under a new moon. I stayed close to the guys and looked straight ahead. I didn't want to know if anyone was following us. I wasn't afraid, but I did feel trepidation. This was not a neighborhood to visit during the day, let alone at night, in total darkness. The only light came from inside the homes that we passed.

We walked into their house, and once again, it was full of people. I grinned, knowing that the message was being accepted. They came because they wanted to hear more.

I found Kris and talked with her for a few minutes. She was wearing a lavender dress that was very attractive. I suggested they name this Wednesday group *Spirit Club*, short for spirituality club.

I told her that I would be coming back only a few more times and asked if she would continue the meetings. Kris liked the idea and promised that she would try. And, by the look in her eye, I was confident that she would succeed. I told her that I would attend from time to time, and she liked that.

"John," said a young man standing next to Kris, "someone recorded the audio of your first two lectures. Can I post them on *YouTube*? I'll title them *Tucson Spirit Club*, with the date of the lecture. I won't include any ads. They will be free."

I mulled it over for a moment. "Sure. I don't have a problem with that."

Kris smiled. "Great. We'll tell everyone on social media to check them out."

Kris organized everyone and then nodded at me to begin.

I was seated in the front of the room, and people were jammed in nearly every empty space. I had only a few feet between me and the audience.

"Okay, this is question night. Who's first?" Several people raised their hands, and I pointed to the fellow wearing a T-shirt with a Republic of Texas flag on the front. Texas had been the first state to secede, and many people respected Texas for being first.

"You state that all experiences are valid. What exactly does that mean?" He sat back down on the floor among the roomful of others who were crowded together.

"Exactly that," I said. "God does not judge an experience as good or bad. God recognizes that *all* experiences are necessary for life to occur. It isn't just us who are experiencing life. God is an integral part of us; there is no separation. Our egos want us to feel separate from God, but that is just the ego's delusion. Our true identity, when all is said and done, is God. Now, if we are God and God is perfection, then any experience that God has is valid. God can do whatever God

Chapter Six - The Spirit Club Grows

wants to do. We are talking about the consciousness that created everything and is everything. Nothing that exists is separate from God."

I scanned the audience looking for familiar faces. Several people stood along the walls. "So, what does this tell us? For one thing, that evil is an illusion. Not only that, but that every event is perfect. The only reason we don't perceive every event as perfect is because we project separation. We think we are separate from God and separate from each other. Once this perception changes, the negative events that are so prevalent today will be gone, or at the very least, rare.

"I know this sounds hard to believe, but society is undergoing a transformation of consciousness. Soon, millions of people will perceive all events that happen in their lives as opportunities for spiritual evolvement. They will feel grateful for being alive at this time, and view everything as either a blessing or an opportunity for spiritual growth.

"Experiences that are currently viewed as negative will be perceived as lessons or opportunities. These so-called negative experiences will be perceived as helping us to evolve. For instance, disharmony evolves into harmony, hate evolves into love, and anger evolves into joy. We are all evolving. It is just not always evident.

"Today, most people are hedonists and think we are here to have fun. In actuality, we are here to serve humanity and learn about love, which is the core of our being. We are not here to have fun. That's just another temptation the ego has in its arsenal. We are here to evolve. Yes, we can live with joy, but that's not the same thing as always trying to have fun. Having fun is often an escape from our objective."

I paused.

"So," Kris asked, while standing against a wall, "you're saying that we're evolving spiritually and that we often use negative experiences for that purpose?"

I looked at her. "In general, yes. Since negativity is so prevalent today, that is what many are using for their lessons. God is intricately involved in our evolution and experiences on this planet. Think of God as *all* of higher selves. This is God's ball game. God chooses the players and the rules."

The group murmured.

"It's naïve for us to think that God gave us this planet and allowed us to use our own free will. God is involved, and God is pulling the strings. For instance, there is not one person here tonight who does not have at least one spirit guide with them right now. Once we recognize how much God is involved in our lives, we can relax. God is in control of everything, and everything happens in a perfectly harmonious way. It may not appear that way on the surface, but in effect that's how it works. The key to life is to not get in the way, but to allow God – our higher self – to make the decisions. Instead of using our egos to direct our lives, we should allow God to show us the way through our hearts.

"But this is not totally accurate. Yes, God is our higher self, but so are we. When we use explanations and definitions that imply separation, then we are not being accurate, because there is no separation between anything. There is only one consciousness. Think of this as the law of one.

"Who else has a question?"

I pointed at Billy, who raised his hand.

"You're heavy, man," Billy said. "You're saying that I'm not supposed to worry, or have any fear, or even feel anger? I don't know if I can do all that."

"No, I didn't say that you are supposed to do anything," I said. "You can do whatever you want, and God will not judge

Chapter Six - The Spirit Club Grows

you for it. You can choose your experiences, and they will all be valid and perfect. However, will they be in harmony with your soul? Perhaps not. To the degree that you have spiritual knowledge – which I am teaching you – the intensity of worry, fear, and anger will dissipate. In their place, will come love, understanding, forgiveness, gratitude, and trust. In other words, at some point, although perhaps not in this lifetime, you will learn spiritual truths. And when you do, you will choose experiences that are aligned with the harmony of your soul.

"Let me give you an example. Once you learn spiritual truth, if someone is angry, you will have compassion for them because they have not yet learned forgiveness. If someone is fearful, you will have compassion, because they have not yet learned trust.

"We are spiritual beings. That is our true identity. That's why feelings of love and forgiveness make us feel warm in our hearts. Everyone feels love and forgiveness to a certain extent. And the more spiritual one becomes, the more intense and encompassing our feelings become."

"What about the government?" Sam asked. "Shouldn't we fight back? We're tired of being treated like criminals."

"What we validate, we empower," I said. "What we resist will persist. The government is powerless. They just don't know it yet. Stop validating them and start ignoring them. I know that, on the surface, this appears contradictory. But our government is the old energy, the old fear-based belief system. Let that energy die on its own. The new energy is our energy; it is a love-based belief system. Our spiritual awareness empowers us. We have the power now.

"We don't have to fight something to change it. We change things just by changing ourselves. Love yourself and love everyone you come into contact with by using loving kindness, and the frequency of love. This will create more change than you can imagine. Spread love, not anger."

"But I'm angry!" Charlie exclaimed loudly.

"Anger comes from fear," I answered calmly. "Why care about what the government is doing? What is there to be angry about? It's all ego. Your ego is telling you that the government is wrong and not treating you fairly. This is a judgment. Fear is actually self-inflicted pain, because, when we're afraid, we're denying our divinity. And when we deny our divinity, we feel pain in our hearts. Thus, when we judge the government as wrong, we inflict pain on ourselves.

"The attitude of an enlightened being is, 'I'm eternal and so is everyone else.'" I paused. "Do you see? When we become enlightened, it no longer matters what is happening in our lives. Why? Because everything is perceived as perfection."

Sam exhaled deeply. "I don't know if I can wrap my mind around that."

Kris raised her hand. "I keep hearing you say that we create our own lives. Can you explain what you mean?"

I paused in contemplation while looking at Kris. "We create everything that happens to us through our beliefs and intent. It's very complicated, and I understand it only in general terms, but I will try to explain."

I looked at Kris as I spoke. "The best place to start is birth. When we're born, at the moment of our first breath, our current life blueprint is created. This blueprint is literally the map of our life. It is based on a lot of factors. One is astrology, which is the alignment of the planets when we took our first breath. Myself, I have the sun in Pisces in the tenth house, Cancer rising, moon in Sagittarius in the sixth house, and so on.

"Astrology is very accurate. It's actually a science that the scientific world refuses to acknowledge. Any astrologer

Chapter Six – The Spirit Club Grows

now knows a lot about me from what I just said. Astrology can explain only one facet of us. And we're much more complicated than the alignment of the planets at our birth. But astrology is real and is a major part of our soul blueprint."

I paused and smiled at a teenage girl sitting in front, who had been paying attention throughout.

"Another part of our blueprint is our past lives, for we all incarnate with a long history. This isn't the first incarnation for anyone in this room. In fact, anyone here tonight most likely has incarnated at least a hundred times, and likely more than five hundred. From these many incarnations, we build a history. This history is our journey of experiencing a myriad of lessons. Thus, when we're born, we come with a contract. The contract can be broad or narrow, but it entails some form of agreement with our higher self. This is an agreement to learn certain lessons in order for the soul to evolve. No one is born without a contract. Everyone in this room has a reason to be here, and that is your contract, whatever it may be."

I gestured with my hands. "We're all on a long journey to find enlightenment. If we only knew how long, we would be amazed. Once we decide to start a reincarnation cycle, we're in it for the long haul. In other words, there is no reneging on the commitment. Once we commit to experiencing a reincarnation cycle, we must complete it. We must learn the final lesson, which is enlightenment."

"What is a reincarnation cycle?" asked Kris.

"Before I answer, let me finish your first question. The blueprint literally encompasses all of the possible futures we can have. Thus, we know in advance everything that can happen. Life is really on rewind. Everything that is happening has already happened. Before we are born, we actually view the future that has already happened. It's all playback. Nothing new is going to happen tomorrow.

"The best book on this subject is *Journey of Souls*, by Michael Newton. It is one of my all-time favorite books. Once you read this book, you will understand how God can see all of our choices interacting with each other. Then God plays with the energy and makes everything occur in perfect harmony, even if we can't perceive it as such. This is where our beliefs and thoughts come into play. God hears our thoughts and reacts accordingly. Thus, we are creating it all in concert with God, who is the great maestro.

"So, our beliefs are somewhat hardwired into us before we are born. We change them occasionally, and when we do, our lives change. So, if you want a new life, change your beliefs. However, because our beliefs are somewhat decided before birth, and our higher self has a contract that it wants completed, our ability to change our beliefs is constrained. This is why life is so hard, and why it's so difficult to change our lives."

I paused. In the back, Billy said, "Wow, that's heavy."

I laughed. "Yeah, it kind of makes your head spin. Okay, let's talk about reincarnation. Fortunately, a group of souls taught us about this in the 1970s and 1980s. That group was called Michael, and they released the Michael Teachings. The Teachings were channeled over a period of years. First, through a Ouija board, and then consciously channeled. The definitive published Teachings were written in two volumes by Chelsea Quinn Yarbro. Another good source is on the Internet at Michael Teachings dot com.

"Anyway, the Teachings revealed that one lifetime isn't that big a deal. So, you can all relax and quit taking your lives so seriously. One cycle can last anywhere from fifty incarnations to over five hundred. During one cycle, we learn approximately thirty-five major lessons. Each life is usually spent on one lesson, although we can finish one lesson and

Chapter Six - The Spirit Club Grows

begin another, or work on multiple lessons during a single lifetime.

"I'm a fifth-level old soul. I learned this through a reading by a Michael channel. I also found out that my current role is Priest-Scholar. There are seven roles, and we can choose a combination of these if we desire. I will briefly describe each role in terms of orientation. *Server*: oriented toward helping others. *Priest*: oriented toward spiritual issues. *Artisan*: oriented toward creating things. *Sage*: oriented toward entertaining others. *Warrior*: oriented toward accomplishing. *King*: oriented toward ruling. *Scholar*: oriented toward learning.

"Isn't it interesting that when we see someone after a lengthy separation, they are usually the same as before? The reason that people seem to stay the same is that we're born with a blueprint, a role, a horoscope, a numerology pattern, and a belief system. All of these limit our ability to change. Thus, we don't change much during a single lifetime.

"Astrology, numerology, and the Michael Teachings give us a bit of understanding about our soul blueprints, but there are also other issues. The biggest is God's grand plan. In essence, we're all in a grand play, and God is the director. We do not really have free will. God is in charge. This is God's play, and our role has already been cast.

"But we know, before we're born, all the possible scripts that God will use. This is where free will comes in and our ability to choose from various options. We select the time we will be born, our parents, and the potential people we will come into contact with. We set things in motion. We set the potential in motion. This is our soul blueprint, and *we* have created it."

I stretched and smiled at the elderly lady seated directly in front of me. She smiled back warmly.

"Okay," I said, "now let's get back to your first question, Kris. We create our experiences based on our current beliefs, and those beliefs come from our blueprint. They are also impacted by the grand plan, by God's play. And because God is an integral part of our lives, God can impact our beliefs. That's why everything is happening with perfection, because God is involved.

"Right now, the beliefs that we hold create our future, and our collective future. And as I stated, those beliefs are from our soul blueprints, and also from our connection with God. How all of this works, I don't exactly know. But I do know that each of us is very powerful, and that we are creating our own lives."

The elderly lady raised her hand. She must have been at least eighty. "I don't have much time left," she said smiling. "Are you saying that I have to hurry up and learn all this stuff?"

I laughed. "I'm glad you asked. The answer is no, absolutely not. Spiritual growth is a very slow process that takes many incarnations. In each life, we learn a blip. That is, we learn very little during one lifetime. Actually, there is nothing to learn in this life. All there is to do is experience.

"So, hurry up? No. There is nothing to achieve. We need only to *be*. I suggest taking life one day at a time, without expectation, and not trying to control the outcome. Take what comes to you and go where your heart desires. P'taah says to do what makes your heart sing."

I paused and scanned the room. "Isn't that beautiful?" Several people nodded in agreement.

"I know that I talk a lot about spiritual knowledge and the ideals of spiritual wisdom, but this information isn't for everyone, and doesn't have to be for everyone." I paused and looked at the elderly lady. "It might be for you. And it might

Chapter Six - The Spirit Club Grows

not. In many respects, I'm teaching those who have a hunger for spiritual wisdom and the expansion of their spiritual consciousness. I'm helping those who are ready for this teaching; those who want to climb a few steps up the spiritual ladder. In no way are these teachings for everyone. Living a spiritual path with a relationship with your higher self is not an easy ordeal. It's a grind and requires commitment and loyalty."

I looked around the room as I continued.

"Again, it isn't for everyone to learn spiritual knowledge in this lifetime, and that's okay. Everyone's time will come. Maybe not in this lifetime, but in another. Eventually, everyone will learn about spiritual knowledge. These talks are like a primer. When the time comes for you to learn such concepts, you'll be more prepared.

"Spirituality of the future won't be group-based. There won't be organized religions. The spirituality of the future will be individual-based. How one person chooses to believe will be their right. Everyone will be allowed to have their own beliefs, and to pursue their own spirituality. So, don't think that there is pressure to learn what I am talking about. Take what you need and leave the rest."

"That sounds good," said the elderly woman. "I have another question. When can we expect things to get better?"

"We have a ways to go, at least a few more years. We still have more trauma ahead. But, rest assured, the coming new civilization will be wondrous. I suggest that we wait for it with a sense of expectant joy. No matter how bad it gets, we all need to have a sense of expectation. And for you, I hope you're here to experience the birth of the next civilization."

She smiled.

I looked at my watch. "All right, one last question."

Kris raised her hand. "Lately, I seem to be in a constant state of anxiety, and I can't seem to relax. Or, when I can relax, it never seems to last. Is there anything I can do?"

I responded with a mock frown. "And I thought that my last question was going to be easy." The crowd laughed.

"Kris, you're plagued with the same malady that many have. You're caught in the illusion of this world. You believe that this world is real and that it is not divinely ordered. You are perceiving separation. You feel separation between yourself and God, and separation between yourself and those around you.

"Earlier, I spoke about how we come into this life with a blueprint, and that we get exactly what we need. That is what you need to recognize to alleviate your anxiety. You need to trust that everything that happens in your life is supposed to happen. You need to trust in the perfection, and know that everything is happening for a purpose, and part of that purpose is an important lesson that you need to learn.

"If this world is divinely ordered, and I believe it is, then we should trust our lives and live with joy in our hearts. I have a checklist that I read every morning to remind myself how I should live my life. I will give you part of it, the ten rules:

1. Acknowledge the Perfection. Recognize that everything is divinely ordered.
2. Be Grateful, Be Humble. Life is a gift, and we should treat it as such.
3. Enjoy the Ride. We can either choose to be happy and enjoy our lives, or not.
4. Live Content. Never want more than you already have.
5. Live Pure. Avoid temptation and the seven deadly sins.
6. Live Simply. In a world of limited natural resources, there is no need to be extravagant.

Chapter Six - The Spirit Club Grows

7. Stay Healthy. Eat nutritious food and exercise. Maintaining your health helps not just yourself, but everyone else.
8. Stay on the Path. Achieve your contract.
9. Stay Present. Quiet your chattering mind.
10. Use Loving Kindness. Be gentle, sensitive to the needs of others.

"Kris, I'll bring you one of my books that have my checklist, and you can make copies for anyone who wants one. Then you can all read the list every morning, and it should help with your anxiety."

Kris smiled and nodded her head.

"In addition to this checklist, there are some other things to be aware of in your daily lives. Try not to react to the events in your life, instead try to respond. This is not easy and takes practice.

"The key to not reacting is to be grounded in the present moment and not caught in the illusion of this life. When you are reacting to the events in your life, you are taking things too personally and not trusting God. Instead of reacting, you need to be accepting. You need to remain neutral, with a quiet mind. The ego is going to scream at you to take things personally. Guess what? You don't have to react. It's a choice, and one choice is to remain calm."

I paused and scanned the room. "Nine times out of ten, when you react to a traumatic experience, it is the ego directing your life. If your emotions and anxiety are rising, it is because you're judging your life experiences as good or bad. However, if you quiet your busy mind, you can respond to the environment using your higher self. Your heart-center is the gateway to your higher self. By listening to your heart, you can feel the presence of God in your life.

"You want to feel with your heart and get out of your head. More specifically, you want to quiet your mind, which will open your heart. When you are reacting with anxiety, the source is your ego and chattering mind. When you are responding with your heart, that is your soul.

"The next time you feel your emotions rising, don't react. Instead, quiet your mind, and allow yourself the ability to respond with your heart. Try to find where the emotion is coming from. Inevitably, it will be from your chattering ego. If you can't do it before you react, then do it later, after your emotional reaction. Try to understand why you reacted. After some practice, you'll learn to remain calm, and you'll begin to respond better to the traumatic events in your life."

I stood. "Thanks, Kris. That was a good question to end on. I hope everyone had a good time. I know I did."

The group applauded, and I smiled.

Chapter Seven

Denver

Two weeks later, I was traveling on a train to Denver. I would be speaking at another New Life Expo and visiting family and friends. Colorado was becoming a popular place to live. It seemed as if everyone was moving there. Even today, the train was full of travelers from California, and I surmised that most of them had one-way tickets.

I don't know what it was, although I suppose it was destiny. People began flocking to Colorado after 2025. Word got out that Colorado was the place to go. Once people began moving there, the area began to take on a new character. It wasn't long before the new arrivals outnumbered the natives.

This is where the new humanity was being born. People moving to Colorado weren't interested in maintaining their old living standards. They arrived with a newfound degree of cooperation and humanity, and a desire to try something different. They came with the understanding that sharing was imperative. There was a new attitude among them.

I personally knew many people who had moved there. Colorado was tempting everyone to come join them. Once society began to crumble, people began to realize that we had to start over, and what better way to start over than to move?

And God played a part in the mass migration. The weather had changed dramatically in the last few years. Cold winters were no longer the norm. It was not uncommon to find sixty-degree days in December and January. Winters had shortened from five months to four. This weather change provided ideal farming conditions. The result was that Colorado not only fed itself, but many other states, as well.

At the turn of the century, the population in Colorado was four million. Today, there are ten million, and it is still growing. Most of the growth has been east of Denver, on the plains. People have been creating their own communities and living off the land. They aren't necessarily trying to rebuild society. They are simply trying to survive and live a simple life.

As I suspected, most of the people got off the train in Denver. The migration was in full swing. I made my way to find a taxi. I considered walking the three miles to the hotel, but I didn't know how safe it was downtown.

The taxi driver had a cellular phone that he rented inside his cab. I asked the rate and was surprised at how reasonable it was. A local call was only one dollar a minute. So, I asked for the phone and called Tina.

"Hello," she answered.

"Tina, babe. It's John. I'm in town."

"Hi, darlin'. Where are you staying?"

I smiled. "At the Marriott. How about dinner in an hour?"

"I'll be there. Do you have a room yet?"

"No. I'll wait for you in the bar."

"Okay, see ya."

Tina and I had been friends for several years. We knew each other so well that it didn't take many words to communicate. You might say we were on the same wavelength.

Tina was the person I called when I needed someone to talk to, which wasn't often. But when I needed advice, or

Chapter Seven - Denver

felt like leaning on someone's shoulder, it was hers. She was a Libra, with Scorpio rising and a Scorpio moon. Libras are incredible at seeing all sides of an argument, and Scorpio is one of the most powerful signs. It's not easy to hide your secrets from them. Scorpio represents the combination of a powerful will and mastery over one's emotions. Because we are all emotional beings, Scorpios have an advantage over the rest of us. Thus, a strong Libra/Scorpio horoscope, creates a powerful personality.

I was in awe of Tina. Her powerful mind ran circles around mere mortals. And her biting wit, along with a desire to put people in their place, was a sight to behold. I had seen her embarrass so many people that I quit counting the occasions. She would spot a weakness, and boom, there went the stinger. To put it mildly, you had to be careful what you said around her.

With all of the Scorpio in her chart, Tina was very sexual and liberated. I never knew what she was going to say in regard to sexuality. She was comfortable with hers and, if you weren't, she could make you squirm. After a few margaritas, it wasn't past Tina to ask a few provocative questions. When I was with Tina, I always expected sexual connotations in her vocabulary.

She called me "darlin'," and I called her "Tina babe." But we were strictly friends. She didn't even like to talk about spirituality, although she did read my books. She preferred to talk about life, and I enjoyed talking about life with her. But more than anything else, I just liked hanging out with her.

I put my luggage in my room and made my way to the bar. It wasn't long before Tina arrived. I got up with a big smile and hugged her.

"Hi, there," she said. "How was your trip?"

"No problems. How have you been?"

"Good. Tell me about Tucson," she said, as she sat down.

"Everything has been okay. Water problems from time to time, but nothing we can't handle. The government has been staying on the outskirts, leaving us alone. As long as they stay out of town, I'm not going to move. I like our little community."

"You should come here. Tucson is a mess, and it's not going to get better." She was baiting me. She always tried to get me to move to Colorado.

"Yeah, I know. But, like I said, I like it there."

Tina shook her head. "You're stubborn. Your sister lives here. I live here. Some of your cousins live here. I could go on. Who do you know in Tucson? What is it about that place? I know it's not Julie; she would leave in a second. Look at what's happening here. We both know it's interesting. People are living off the land, sharing what they have with each other. The sense of community that's developing is nothing short of astonishing. New Age spirituality is thriving. This is where you can do some good."

I refused to take the bait and argue with her. "If I'm supposed to be here," I said calmly, "I'll be here. Right now, I'm supposed to be in Tucson."

"And you plan to stay there?" she asked.

"For the time being."

"Okay," she sighed, accepting my decision. "Well, I had to get that off my chest. Let's change the subject.

"There's a small group of Hopi Indians here helping people live off the land. There's only about thirty or forty of them, but they're having a big impact.

"They're teaching people how to farm with very little fertilizer and no pesticides. Many people call it natural farming. It's catching on. It's amazing to see these Indians interacting with the local population. They're like saviors.

Chapter Seven - Denver

They're so friendly and warm-hearted. I cry when I see them; it's so wonderful. And not only are they teaching us about farming, but many other things as well. People are learning how important it is to work with nature and not against it. And many are learning about the spirituality of the Hopi."

Tina paused, and then continued in a more serious tone. "Did you know the Hopi believe that God gave them a tablet, much like he had given to Moses?"

I nodded. "Their history is fascinating."

"I don't know exactly what's written on the tablet," she said, "but it's to the effect that they're to stay on Black Mesa in the Four Corners region and nurture the land. It also states that Black Mesa is their land, given to them by God. What's incredible is that they believe it. The Hopi have lived on Black Mesa for thousands of years, and they have never armed themselves. They're a peaceful and spiritual people. In fact, they are the spiritual masters of the Native Americans."

"Have you heard of the *Book of the Hopi*?" I asked. "Or the prophecy of the Hopi?"

Tina shook her head, and her eyes lit up in anticipation.

"The Hopi knew what was going to happen to America," I said. "They knew that this was going to be a very tumultuous period. The *Book of the Hopi* was published in the 1980s, years before the chaos began. The book explained their prophecy and foretold of the coming turmoil. The Hopi have known of this prophecy for thousands of years, long before the existence of the United States. They've been waiting for this time period. Now their mission is to help with the transition, so that they can have their way of life back."

I became more animated. "Nobody knew about the history of the Hopi until the 20th century, because they kept to themselves. They're peaceful and do not fight their oppressors. When the government started mining their ancient lands on Black Mesa, they didn't complain, although they told the governor of Arizona that it was their land and that they hadn't given their permission.

"The Hopi have always kept to themselves. Now that the transition has begun, however, they're wandering away from Black Mesa and helping us. They know that we will soon all live together in peace."

"Yeah," Tina said. "The Hopi have a lot to offer. It appears that people are beginning to realize this. You know what I find fascinating? The Hopi have experienced government tyranny all their lives. That experience provides them with a perspective that we don't have. People are drawn to them because the government is now trying to control us, too, just like they did the Indians. I think this is why people feel such an affinity with them."

I nodded. "What's happening here is not that unexpected to me. I expected the Native Americans to help during the transition. They understand that we are all one. They understand the scripture, John 14:20: 'I am in my father, and ye in me, and I in you.' The Native American culture is much more spiritual than our own. We need their knowledge during these times. What's happening now was inevitable."

I paused for a second to reflect, then continued. "Their culture and spirituality are helping us, but that's not where we're headed. Technology is our future, and that's not what the Native Americans are about. They are only one source of knowledge that is helping us."

"There's a new sense of idealism sweeping across Colorado," Tina said. "People are beginning to believe that everything is going to work out, that no matter what happens, we'll make it work. This idealism is genuine. People believe that we can help each other. And not only that, but that we *will* help each other.

Chapter Seven – Denver

"A new can-do attitude is taking root. People here are learning that each of us is only as secure as the group. A new mindset is taking hold. In fact, I'm beginning to feel that way myself."

She paused and smiled. "People are forgetting about their material possessions. Their overriding concerns are turning toward society and humanity. The new attitude is, 'What can I do to help?' I'm sensing that more and more."

"Indeed," I said. "People are realizing that when we separate into diverse interest groups, society degenerates. The focus on self-interest hasn't provided the spiritual answers or created a harmonious civilization. Now there is a swing away from the focus on self-interest and individuality, and it is producing a focus on the group. As you say, this focus is creating a sense of idealism that we can do it together."

"You're so smug," she said. "You say all of this as if you think it might happen. But, deep down, you don't have any doubts, do you?"

I laughed. "No, but I meet so few who grasp what's going to happen, that I've learned not to be so adamant. I give people small sips instead of big gulps. Most people can only handle sips."

"So, we're going to build a more peaceful civilization?" she asked.

I nodded. "Yes, we're going to create peace on Earth. That's what the transition is all about. We're creating a new civilization, which will be much more harmonious. Although for many, it will be somewhat boring and less exciting than in the past, where striving for achievement was the ultimate goal.

"Until recently, America has been an exciting place to live," I continued. "Where we're headed is a new era, and it'll be much more spiritual than it is today. Experiences will be primarily positive and harmonious. This planet is evolving upward spiritually and is about to take a quantum leap. Once that occurs, negative experiences will be curtailed. Then, the duality that provided rich experiences will no longer exist. News reports will no longer be filled with people breaking laws, economic woes of the unfortunate, or incessant tragedies."

"You sound sad," Tina said, with a look of bewilderment.

"Yeah, I get this way when I'm nostalgic. This was a great country, and it's sad to think that it's coming to an end. We had such potential, and we squandered it. The experiences available to us were so rich and full, and our standard of living was so high. We created a wonderful nation, maybe not for everyone, but for many."

"We did squander it, didn't we?" Tina said in a somber tone.

I nodded. "Why didn't America last another hundred years? Why not peace on Earth with our current civilization? These questions haunt me. We had the potential, but we failed. Our demise was from the same thing that doomed Atlantis. We ignored our soul and listened to our ego. The false ego brought us all down."

Tina laughed. "I know that my ego is my nemesis."

"We all know that, Tina." I smiled at her playfully. "But don't stop being yourself. It's too late for regrets, anyway. The civilization we grew up with is gone."

Tina and I had dinner, and then parted. She repeated her desire for me to move my family to Colorado, even though she knew where I stood. I told her that I would be in touch.

* * * * *

The next day, I visited my younger sister and her family in a community twenty miles east of Denver. The previous

Chapter Seven - Denver

year when I visited, they had more than a thousand people in her community. Now the nearby population had grown into the millions.

On the bus, on my way to see my sister, I glanced at the tent communities all along the road. Tents of all sizes filled the landscape. Outside of the Denver area, tent communities continued for miles along Highway 70 East. The first tent community had taken root in 2025. The next one was built beside it shortly after, and then the pattern continued. I knew that if I took the bus far enough, I would see new communities all the way to the Nebraska border.

These communities were groups of people camping together. They had water and electricity, but only enough to survive. Each was rationed a daily amount of water and electricity, depending on the size of the community. There were very few buildings. The communities were primarily made up of tents, although there were many tables and canopies.

At my sister's community, they had a huge tent where people ate. The tent was rectangular and open on the sides. It was approximately one hundred and fifty feet by fifty feet. Underneath the tent were forty large tables, and each seated twenty people, so eight hundred could eat there. It was a huge picnic area. Many communities had large tents such as this.

The main reason I didn't live in Colorado was because there wasn't as much to do as in Tucson. I felt the quality of life was better in Tucson. If I were here, I probably would be working on a farm, which was the most common job available. Farm jobs were somewhat plentiful, although seasonal. Most people who owned farms allowed people to work for a portion of the crop. Then, there were some communities that owned their own farms and tilled their own land. Those communities ended up supporting many others.

Barter, gold, and a new digital currency issued by the Colorado Territory were the most common forms of exchange. Colorado had seceded from the United States in 2028. Since then, the dollar was no longer used in Colorado, although dollars could be exchanged for the new state currency. Most exchange was done with the new state currency, which was partially backed with gold.

I got off the bus and made my way to my sister's community. Four-man tents were neatly aligned row after row, separated by only a few yards. The area was a bright collage of different-colored tents. I walked to the main tent and found several people seated there in conversation.

"Hi, my name is John Randall. I'm looking for my sister, Shelby. Shelby Weldon."

One of the ladies smiled and got up from her chair immediately. "John! Good to see you again. I'm Alice Bailey. We met the last time you were here. Come, I know where to find your sister."

I followed Alice back to the rows of tents, and she pointed out my sister's. Shelby was inside her tent, reading with her son, James. She put down the book and came out to see me, and my nephew was right behind her.

"John! You made it!" Shelby exclaimed with her usual enthusiasm. "How are Julie and Kate?" We hugged. And then I hugged James.

"They're good. How's everything here?"

She immediately mentioned my brother-in-law and my niece. "Okay. Todd has Brit with him. He's working on a farm a few miles away. How long are you going to stay?"

"Just tonight and tomorrow. I have to get back to Denver tomorrow night for a lecture."

"All right. But I hope you aren't tired, because we really need you to talk tonight. There's been a raging debate lately

Chapter Seven - Denver

that we need to start building permanent communities, with elected officials and police and everything else! Many people believe that we need to emulate the communities we left. You know how I feel. If they want to live that way, they can move back to town!" Shelby was very expressive, moving her hands and talking quickly.

I grimaced. "Shelby, you know I don't like to get involved in politics. What exactly do you want me to talk about?"

"Just talk about spirituality; why we're here; and, where society is headed. You don't have to say a word about the debate. You don't even have to mention it. But your words will help those of us who know the futility of trying to rebuild society the way it was. It's time to think, to ponder, and to understand what's happening. Wouldn't you agree?"

"To each his own," I said. "If people want to build a permanent community, I don't see anything wrong with it. And if they don't, that's fine, too. Each of us has our own ideas on how to live."

"Oh, you Pisces!" Shelby exclaimed. "You drive me nuts sometimes! Can't you make a stand on anything?"

I laughed. "Look, there's no right way. Our collective beliefs will decide the outcome. You can choose to fight for your desire to not build, or you can passively allow it to happen. Either way, the community's collective beliefs are going to decide as a group which option to choose."

"I still want you to talk tonight," she pleaded. "At least you know the future better than those who want to build so adamantly. I would at least like them exposed to the futility of the past."

I looked at James. "Let's go find Brit."

As James and I walked away, I turned to Shelby. "Sure, I'll speak. How can I say no?" I smiled, and she smiled back.

Spirit Club

* * * * *

Just a few hours later, our meeting began. I was surprised at the large turnout on such a short notice. Word had spread during dinner that a New Age speaker would be talking under the main tent, and the tent was crowded with more than one hundred people. There was a lot of diversity; all races and all ages could be seen. I spoke from a raised platform, using a handheld microphone.

"Most of you do not know who I am," I said. "My name is John Randall. I'm Shelby Weldon's brother. She's lived here, in this community, for nearly two years. Today, when I showed up to visit, she asked if I would give a talk tonight. And you know how it is with family when they ask for a favor. It's hard to say no." I grinned, and the audience laughed.

"I'm a metaphysical writer. This weekend, I'll be speaking at the New World Expo in Denver. One of the topics I'll be talking about is the future. I'm a bit of a futurist. I've been doing research regarding the future since 1989, and my research has been fruitful. What we are experiencing now isn't a surprise to me. I expected this to occur.

"The list of sources who predicted the collapse of this country are numerous: Nostradamus, Edgar Cayce, the Hopi, the Mayans, P'taah, Kryon, Kirael, Abraham, Lazarus, St. Germain, Bashar, Bartholomew, Chet Snow, Ruth Montgomery, Moria Timms, Dolores Cannon, Gordon-Michael Scallion, the Gulf Breeze Six, and many others. The list is long. Most of this information came through in the 1980s and 1990s, preparing the world for this great shift that we are now experiencing.

"All of these sources foresaw the events that are transpiring today. None of them had it exactly right, but they all foresaw the decline of our civilization during our lifetime and the unprecedented earth changes. Not only did they predict the decline, but also a transformation into a New Age and peace on Earth. They foresaw a transformation so abrupt that the prior civilization would literally be replaced by a spiritual New Age.

"We have witnessed the decline of what was a great nation. I don't know how much further it will fall before we begin our ascent, but the rise is imminent."

I paused and looked at the audience. "How many of you expect our new society to resemble the past? Look at how drastically things have changed. Look at our social structures. Everything is breaking down or has broken down. And the decline still hasn't stopped. Nor shall it stop for a few more years. We're in a spiral of decline, and we still have a way to go before we will start to rebuild.

"The next few years are going to be much like this year. In fact, I don't foresee any real progress until after 2035. We're going to have to be patient and allow the spiritual transformation to unfold.

"We're in the process of making a very dramatic jump. We're changing from a civilization that basically was living in spiritual ignorance, which was third dimensional energy, to a civilization living with more spiritual awareness in fourth dimensional energy.

"By the time we get to 2050, civilization will be back on its feet. Technologically, we've been stagnating for a few years. I would expect that to continue for another decade. By 2050, however, we will be advanced technologically once again. Soon, we will be living in space and using clean energy. Thus, our future is technology, but it will take a while to rebuild the infrastructure.

"Once we get to 2050, our spirituality will have taken a quantum leap. And over the next few years, our spirituality will change dramatically. By 2035, we will have taken great strides. The degree of love, humanity, and spiritual awareness that will exist in a few short years will be astounding compared to where we are today. And here is something to ponder: our spiritual awareness will continue to expand. Our potential is now unlimited. People with the same abilities as Jesus will not be that uncommon to encounter in a few years.

"What does it mean to change from an ego-based, material-based society into a spiritually-based society? In a word, it means harmony. We won't necessarily create paradise, or heaven on earth, but we will create harmony. We're going to advance both technologically and spiritually. And, as we evolve, we'll get along with each other. There will be harmony. That, I promise you, is our destiny.

"We're going to go from one extreme, which was ego and materialism, to another, which will be spirituality and love. When the pendulum swings, it swings to the degree of the previous swing. The planet made a big swing to the negative about ten thousand years ago. Now it's swinging back to the positive. This will take four generations to complete. This type of a swing from spiritual ignorance to spiritual enlightenment is rare in the cosmos. Most planets don't make such major transformations. In many respects, what we're doing is very exciting. The end result, will be a planet with a lot of harmony, which is the norm for most planets."

I paused and stared at my niece, Brit, in the first row, as I collected my thoughts. I had told her many times what I was about to say next.

"In a few short years, the extraterrestrials will land. And who do you think they will communicate with?" I looked at Brit.

She smiled and said, "The New Agers."

Chapter Seven – Denver

"Yes, the New Agers. They will want to talk with the people who are creating the changes. They will want to talk to the people who are aware of the direction we're headed. And, my friends, that is us."

Many in the audience were murmuring. Some agreed and some disagreed. Those who agreed showed their approval with smiles and vocal outbursts.

I continued. "Today, we're all learning about how to create a new civilization. The reason this transition has been so abrupt was to force us to let go of the past, especially beliefs that did not serve us. That's what we're doing. We're having a period of contemplation, a transition period. Many of us are pondering deep questions. Such as, where are we heading? What is the world going to look like in a few years?

"I have given some clues to the answers to these questions. We are headed towards peace on Earth and a civilization based on love and harmony. To create such a place, we need to use the highest values known to mankind. These values are what evolved souls use to live their lives. Let me list them:

1. They are selfless and egoless.
2. They are highly compassionate and sensitive to the needs of others.
3. They are gentle and use loving kindness.
4. They are fearless and trusting that the world is divinely ordered.
5. They live by integrity and are incredibly humble.
6. They live simple lives and stay in the present moment.
7. They are grateful and content.
8. They are courageous and determined.
9. They acknowledge the law of one.

10. They are spirit-led and heart-led.

"Those need to be the values of the new civilization that we are trying to create. I take that back; those *are* the values of the civilization that is about to arise."

I stopped. "Well, that's all I have for tonight. Thank you for coming. Be grateful and live with love and joy in your heart. We're heading toward a beautiful age. Feel fortunate to be alive at this time. We have a front row seat in this grand drama."

They applauded politely. Several people approached me to ask questions. We found an empty table to sit down, and I talked with them for another hour.

Chapter Eight

Federal Task Force

The next day, I went early to the New World Expo in Denver so that I could help my agent, Stan, set up. He amazed me with his consistency. Being a Virgo, he always made sure the little things got done. If there was one thing to describe Stan, it was his fastidiousness.

I sat at the booth all morning, signing books and talking with people. Tina came with her son, Jeremy. They promised to come to my lecture at noon. I also saw several old friends whom I hadn't seen in years; that was always a welcome experience.

Vance Davis came by, and we talked about the Gulf Breeze Six prophecies. In his book, *Unbroken Promises*, he described the experience he had in 1990 with five other people in military intelligence. They experimented with a Ouija board and had success contacting discarnate souls on the other side. They became famous when they were arrested in Gulf Breeze, Florida, in July 1990, for being AWOL from the military. They made national headlines because, at a news briefing, the military said that the six were members of a religious cult that expected the world to end.

What's fascinating about this case was that the military released all six with honorable discharges. They could have been court-martialed for desertion and sent to jail. When publicity exploded, however (the story was covered by *CNN* and *USA Today*), the military released them two weeks after their arrest.

Even more fascinating was that the discarnate souls had helped the group plan their desertion and had told them that they would not go to jail. After their arrest and release, the group went underground and didn't speak publicly until 1993. Vance became one of the voices for them. He wrote a book and began giving lectures.

What did the discarnate souls tell the Gulf Breeze Six? First, a probable future for the planet. The accuracy of the prophecies, made public in 1993, became legendary. They weren't 100 percent correct, but they were uncannily accurate. The prophecies foretold of the coming breakup of the United States and the economic chaos. When first made public, the prophecies were shrugged off by the average citizen. Vance Davis did not become a household name.

One prophecy I hoped very much would prove inaccurate was the prediction of the government becoming tyrannical. This prophecy predicted that, after the economic collapse, the government would use its power to control the populace. In effect, the government would take away the rights of the many to protect the status quo. The status quo was the old system, whereby the corporations, military, and politicians made the rules.

In other words, the prophecy predicted that our freedoms would be taken away. This prophecy stated that the military would become more repressive than the Russians had been during the height of communism! I didn't want this prophecy to be accurate. For many cities today, however, we couldn't get through the day without contact with military personnel. Why were they occupying our cities? They claimed they were helping to keep the peace and to avoid anarchy. In reality,

Chapter Eight - Federal Task Force

they were there to keep the power vested with those who had it before the economic collapse.

Fortunately, many states, especially in the West, had already seceded from the union and become independent territories. Even so, the military had a presence, which was primarily felt on the outskirts of cities. The government didn't want to start a civil war, which would have happened if the military had attempted to take control of the free territories.

The federal government refused to abandon its military bases and government-owned lands in the free territories. Thus, harassment and contact occurred all the time between the military and civilians. It became a game of cat and mouse, and many people were arrested, supposedly for national security reasons.

The military believed that they represented and protected Americans. In fact, since the new terrorism laws that resulted from the 9/11 attacks in 2001, anyone could be arrested as an enemy combatant, and held indefinitely without a trial.

Freedom and human rights were precarious. Being stopped and questioned by military personnel was an everyday occurrence throughout the nation. In the West, makeshift detention centers held thousands of American prisoners. They were mostly political prisoners. Many of them had done nothing other than protest against tyranny.

* * * * *

At noon, I left my Expo booth and went to give my lecture. The large room was packed with over 200 people. I approached the lectern without notes and addressed the crowd.

"Hello, everyone. I'm John Randall. Thanks for coming." I paused and took a drink from a bottle of water that was placed on the lectern for my use.

"The first thing I want to talk about is the wonderful shift in awareness that is taking place today. When society began its descent a few years ago, people focused on fear and devastation. Their response was, 'Oh my God, I'm going to lose all of my stuff!'" I paused, and the audience laughed.

"That reaction came from our focus on self, and society's focus on individuality. Today, our focus has changed. Now we are focusing on the group. This new awareness is causing people to help each other and to learn how to live together as a group. A new sense of idealism and humanity is beginning to flourish.

"What's happening here in Colorado is wonderful. It's magnificent. Colorado is leading the way, along with Arizona, New Mexico, and Montana. Your state is setting a fine example. You are changing the entire energy of the planet. By focusing on humanity, you are creating experiences here that are sending out positive vibrations all over the world. You are creating an example here that is affecting the world."

I smiled and bowed to let them know I appreciated the work they were doing. Many smiled back.

"Before the descent, society's focus was on ego and self. From this focus, people constantly judged each other. Here in Colorado, you are showing us that judgment is counterproductive. Here, everyone is treated as a human being and an equal. People are loved here, just for being human. You have realized that, unless we learn to accept each other, society will fail."

I paused and scanned the audience.

"What a miracle! What a beautiful shift that is taking place today. Judgment is going away. Who would have ever thought that could happen in our lifetime? Do all of you realize the ramifications of this change?

Chapter Eight - Federal Task Force

"I'm sure many of you feel this difference every day. I know I do. Before, everyone avoided eye contact. Now, everyone wants to look into each other's eyes and share their experiences. On an emotional level, life is much more profound today than before the collapse. We're becoming very emotional because we're sharing love."

"Also, once we stopped judging others, we stopped judging ourselves. Whereas in the past, people were conditioned to judge themselves as lacking, today people are beginning to accept themselves as divinity. This change in focus has unleashed a torrent of self-love across the land. Before the collapse, people could not love themselves. Now that they can, and are also able to love others."

I paused and took another drink of water.

"Today, I bring you good news. The time is quickly approaching when we will become aware, as a civilization, that we *are* God. Soon, we will recognize that there is no separation between us and God. In fact, we're already closer to this awareness than we realize. Many people are already living their lives with this awareness. As this knowledge becomes more pervasive, people will begin to co-create experiences that bring this awareness into everyone's lives. For instance, today, we are talking about it. Tomorrow, we will live it."

I paused. "Does anyone have anything they would like to add to what I've said? There's a microphone up here in front." I pointed toward the microphone, which was in front of the audience and facing the stage.

A lady in the second row rose and made her way to the microphone. She was in her thirties and wore a dress with a collage of bright colors.

"I agree with what you have been saying," she said. "People have changed dramatically in the last few years. I hear people saying things today that I've never heard before. I hear people saying that we shouldn't judge others, because when we do, we're only judging ourselves.

"At first, I wasn't open to this concept. But I respected the people who were saying it, so I continued to listen. Today, I agree with them. We're all one, and when we judge another, we're just judging ourselves. Everything that we see outside of ourselves is only a reflection of who we are. By rejecting something outside of ourselves, we're just rejecting ourselves."

She stopped, and the audience applauded.

"Thank you. That was very nice. Anyone else?"

A young teenager rose and walked to the microphone. He was tall and thin, with light brown hair down to his shoulders. His eyes were penetrating, and I was impressed by his demeanor at such a young age.

"I have learned that we each have access to more knowledge than is in our brain. We can tap into spiritual knowledge through our soul. Everyone has more intelligence than we're given credit for.

"Spiritual knowledge doesn't come from the brain, but from our soul, our spirit consciousness. That's why gurus say that all knowledge is within. They aren't implying that knowledge is in the body, but in the soul. Spirituality is about remembering how to access our spiritual knowledge."

He continued. "So, when I see people in public, I now realize that everyone isn't who they appear. We're much more dynamic and complex than that. The spiritual side of us is hidden. The spiritual knowledge that some people hold can be amazing, yet it can come from the person who cleans this floor tonight after we leave. The very concept of success or achievement has no meaning to me anymore."

Chapter Eight - Federal Task Force

The audience was stunned. He was so young, and yet he talked with such assuredness. Everyone there knew that he was special. The room was silent, with an expectation that he had something to teach us.

He turned to go back to his seat.

"Please, can you stay at the microphone?" I asked. "I have some questions for you." He turned back towards me and waited.

"First of all, you are an old soul and have a lot to offer. Anyone at your age who can speak in front of a large crowd with such knowledge, and so eloquently, has our respect. What's your name?"

"Toby."

"Hi, Toby. Since we're speaking of concepts, have you heard of the concept that we are divine, eternal beings? If yes, what do you think of it?"

"Yeah, I've heard of it," he said. "It corresponds with what you talked about earlier. People can't love themselves because they feel separate from God. If people knew that they were divine, eternal beings, it would be much easier for them to love themselves.

"People invalidate their divinity by believing that they aren't eternal. They view all aspects of self from the perspective that we're mortal. They don't remember that they are eternal. However, this is changing as more people remember."

He waited for me to reply.

"Okay, I have another question," I said. "What about the concept of achievement? Earlier, you said that it has no meaning to you."

Toby gathered his thoughts. "Well, that's the past. That's how society used to be. We're now beyond that, instead, we're now striving for fulfillment in our lives. And this fulfillment doesn't have to be measured in terms of success or achievement. It can be defined in many different ways. If someone has a desire to excel and achieve in certain fields, that's fine. But it's not paramount for everyone to have this attitude. And in no way are certain achievements superior to others. That's the kind of attitude that was prevalent in the past. Before, people were fixated on their identities. People believed that their identities were based on what they achieved. In essence, society was ego-based."

Toby looked back over his shoulder at the audience to see if he should continue, then he turned back to the microphone.

"We must not define each other according to our achievements. If we do, we'll be right back where we were. But I don't think that's going to happen. People are changing. People are beginning to realize that we're all basically the same."

Toby finished and waited for my next question. The audience listened closely and as eagerly as I did.

"Do you ever get angry?" I asked. "And if you do, afterward do you think about why you got angry? Perhaps even of the lesson learned?"

He smiled. "I'm a Scorpio, with the Moon and Mars in Aries, and Sagittarius rising. Aries and Sagittarius are fire signs, so you might say that my emotions heat up a lot. Just yesterday, I was treated rudely, and it was nearly unbearable not to get upset. It's something that I have to deal with all the time."

He shrugged. "In many ways, it's a blessing, because I'm being forced to quiet my chattering mind. Otherwise, my ego will tempt me to get upset. As a Scorpio, I'm able to control my emotions to a certain degree. But if I'm going to learn how to completely control my emotions, I have to quell my ego.

Chapter Eight - Federal Task Force

"Every time I get upset, I know that my ego is the instigator. Lately, I've been trying to create space the minute my emotions take off. I try to create space between my chattering mind and the awareness of my chattering mind. This space allows my soul to enter into the present moment. If I can just get in touch with my soul and create space and observe my thoughts, then the anger will fade.

"A good way to create space is to take your awareness outside of your body and then look back at yourself. For instance, put your awareness up in the corner of the room, looking down at yourself. Then, allow the awareness to just watch and observe what you are thinking. This will create space and allow the soul into the moment.

"I know this may sound strange," he continued, "but sometimes I try to relax and enjoy it, no matter how discordant the experience. However, I can only do this when I step back from the situation and view it from outside my body as a spectator. I literally take my awareness outside of my body. This is very easy to do if you try."

Toby reflected and furrowed his brow. "My biggest problem is that my ego often tricks me and creates trauma in my life. When this happens, I can't create space fast enough, and my emotions heat up. Thus, my ego tricks me into believing the trauma is real.

"My Mars likes to heat up from time to time, and I'm trying to get a handle on it. But, after all, I'm still a kid."

The audience and I laughed.

"Toby, one last question. Have you heard the expression, 'You can transmute fear with trust'? If yes, what would you say about it?"

"Mr. Randall, I thought the last question was always supposed to be easy?"

The audience laughed again.

"Call me John. Do you want an easier one?"

"No, I'll answer it. It's a good question."

"Okay," I said, "but I do have a final easy one. How old are you? And where did you learn all this knowledge?"

"That's two more questions. I'm eighteen, and my mother has been teaching me and my sisters as far back as I can remember. I was reading Jane Roberts when I was eight. I've always read my mom's books. She has a lot.

"Okay, your question. How can we transmute fear with trust? First, we have to recognize that fear and the truth cannot coexist. So, if we are afraid, then the ego is tricking us. Fear is false evidence appearing real. Next, we have to recognize that we are creating our lives. Until we accept the fact that nothing happens that wasn't pre-planned before we were born, we're stuck in fear. However, once we accept all of the events in our lives as divinely ordained, we can expose our fears as ego-based illusions, and that they are either blessings or opportunities for our soul growth.

"It's up to us to recognize that fear is an illusion and that only love is real. One solution is to realize how stupid it is to be afraid and, instead, love yourself as a divine being. However, this does not always work. Sometimes it takes many lessons until we recognize that only the ego can trick us into being afraid.

"One of the best lessons I learned in my life came from my mom. One time she had an obvious unforeseen trauma. I was worried about how she would react and that she would be sad. To my amazement, she wasn't even fazed, and said, 'Everything will be fine.' And you know what? She was right. In her heart, she knew what was important and what wasn't. The ego couldn't trick her."

Toby paused. "In the movie, *Blow*, with Johnny Depp, he uses the line, 'It was perfect,' to describe a point in his life.

Chapter Eight - Federal Task Force

That is the mindset we need to have at all times. His life may not have been perfect in our eyes, but to him it was.

"Fear is always from the ego, which is from believing in the illusion of life. Once we accept that the world is divinely ordered, fear loses its grip. In many ways, we have to change our beliefs so that they align with our true self. It's resistance to aligning with our true self that causes fear. Once we align, love begins to flow." He paused.

"I know all this sounds easy," Toby said, "but it's not. In fact, until we're ready to align with our true self, we align with our ego. One thing that helps us find this alignment is the understanding that our fears come from the ego. The ego is our false identity, and over time, we come to this understanding. In other words, after many lives, we start to understand that we do have a true identity, one that is not afraid. Eventually, we align with this true identity and stop paying attention to our ego. This is when we finally remember who we are, which is God."

I began to clap, and the whole room exploded in applause. Some of the younger people in the audience whistled.

"Toby, thank you for your uplifting words," I said. "It makes me feel good to know that there are people like you out there spreading knowledge."

"Thanks, Mr. Randall." He walked back to his seat.

"Well, that's all the time we have today," I said to the audience. "Remember what Toby taught us. Find an alignment with your true self and you'll never be angry or afraid again. Have a good day."

* * * * *

The next day, I was on a train heading back to Tucson. The train stopped at the border of the Colorado and Utah Territories. Men in black military uniforms boarded the train and questioned everyone. I was asked to present identification and to verbally state my destination and the reason for my trip.

The man who interrogated me carried an assault rifle. His manner implied that he would use it with little provocation. On his sleeve, and on the upper left chest of his uniform, was the emblem of the Federal Task Force (FTF). The emblem was shaped like a three-dimensional box.

The FTF had multiple jurisdictions because, when created in 2025, it supplanted the National Guard, Homeland Security, the FBI, and other national security organizations. The FTF was an all-powerful, national police force, created to oversee martial law and civil unrest. It had turned, however, into a modern-day Gestapo.

The nickname for the FTF was the "Black Guards." Everyone called them this because of their black uniforms, black helicopters, and black vehicles.

One of the interesting things about them was that no one knew who was in charge of the FTF. Was it Washington politicians or the military? There were rumors that Washington had nothing to do with the FTF. If it wasn't Washington, then who was really in charge of them?

In Arizona and Colorado, the FTF remained outside of the cities. In California, which was still part of the union, the FTF had a huge presence and basically controlled that state. When we made trips to Bakersfield to get food, we always had to pass through checkpoints. So far, we had been allowed through because the FTF thought the food was for my restaurant, which was partially true. However, they could stop our food runs at any time.

The one thing that would get me to move to Colorado would be if the FTF took over Tucson, although I didn't think that would happen. The FTF would remain intact for

Chapter Eight - Federal Task Force

only a few more years, and then their power and influence would subside. The FTF was the military's internal arm, and as long as the military had power, the FTF would be around. However, as the federal government faded, so would the military.

After the FTF got off the train, someone in my section couldn't contain his agitation.

"Those bastards! I swear they think we're at war. And exactly who are we at war with? I don't understand the Black Guards. How did this happen in America?"

"You shouldn't talk," said a man near him. "They'll find out and arrest you."

"Should I care?" the agitated man replied intensely. "Look at what's happening to this country. If we don't take back our rights, this country will rot. Somebody has to stand up to them."

No one else spoke. The conversation was getting too dangerous. If there was a spy on the train, and there probably was, it was foolish to speak out in public.

The Black Guards were vigilant in the repression of their enemies. The FTF was at war, a war they had created. Their enemies were those who tried to take away their power. Whoever was behind the FTF knew that the only way they could maintain power was to use power. They also must have known it would get ugly and that internal conflict was inevitable.

"What do you think of the Black Guards?" asked the woman sitting beside me. She was about sixty. She had graying hair and an aura of sadness around her. Her hopes and dreams obviously had been dashed, and she seemed to hold a great deal of pessimism for the current state of affairs.

I looked around to see who was sitting near us. We were virtually alone near the back, so I felt comfortable talking to her. "They're powerless," I said. "They just don't know it yet."

"What do you mean?" she asked.

"We're currently going through a spiritual transformation," I replied in a calm and assuring voice. "In a few years, the Black Guards will be nothing more than a memory. By then, much of the U.S. population will have progressed to a level of spirituality that will no longer allow such a negative environment."

She stared at me, completely perplexed. "How will these so-called spiritually advanced people disarm the Black Guards?" she asked.

"With love."

She looked skeptical. "With love?"

"Yeah," I said. "Right now, people are still fighting back against the FTF. People are angry. When people drop their anger and begin loving the Black Guards, the FTF will put away their weapons."

She laughed. "You have to be kidding."

"Have you read any New Age material?" I asked.

"Oh no," she exclaimed. "That's the work of the devil. I read only the Bible."

"How do you think God will receive me?" I asked.

"I suppose with welcome arms. Do you accept Jesus as your savior?"

I nodded. "As my mentor, if that's the same thing. However, since 1989, most of my reading material has been New Age spirituality, and not the Bible. I've written several New Age books, and I've taught New Age spirituality to thousands of people. Do I seem like someone who is in the clutches of the devil?"

Chapter Eight - Federal Task Force

"No, you don't. You seem like an honorable man. She squinted and looked at me nervously. Why are you telling me this?"

"Because I'm not kidding. We are indeed experiencing a transformation, a spiritual transformation. By the next generation, the Bible will no longer be read. Why? Because it's no longer valid. In fact, it will only keep you from understanding the *truth*. In fact, right now, I'll bet you're feeling lost, and the Bible has not given you the answers to the questions that burden you daily. For instance, do you know who you are? Do you know who God is? Do you know why you're alive?"

"Go on," she said, becoming cautiously interested.

I reached into my travel bag, under my seat, and grabbed one of my books. "This book has sold twenty-three thousand copies. After you finish it, you'll have a glimpse of the transformation that I'm talking about. Here, you can have it."

I handed it to her, and she looked it over slowly and opened the cover. "Thank you. I will read it."

"My pleasure. Even if you currently believe that the Bible has all of the answers, you needn't be afraid to expose yourself to New Age knowledge. Christianity, in its present form, only has a few decades left. Soon, Christianity will have evolved to such an extent that it will barely be recognizable. Many beliefs currently held are going to break down and dissolve. The beliefs that will replace them are New Age beliefs, such as those that I teach."

"And the new beliefs are going to force everyone to put away their weapons?" she asked, with a hint of awe.

"It won't force them, but it will teach people to love each other. For instance, start observing how people change in the next few years. Watch how love expands and eventually leads people, including the Black Guards, to put away their weapons."

"My goodness! That sounds too incredible. What are you saying? That we're headed toward a utopia?" She considered the possibility, and almost smiled.

"Yeah. That's exactly where we're headed. I don't know if utopia is the right word. I prefer to call it a period of harmony, or peace on Earth."

She grew silent. "You sound very confident."

"I've watched the world unfold, and I know where it's going. This isn't just my expectation, but that of millions of people in the New Age community. Read a few other New Age books. Educate yourself and watch the world evolve. We're right in the middle of it. All of the major changes will happen over the next few years. We're going to experience an incredible transformation, although it will take four generations to complete, so the initial changes might be somewhat tentative."

"What are the new beliefs? I know that you believe in reincarnation," the woman said, with curiosity.

I hesitated, surprised by her interest. "Yes, we do. We also believe that there is no separation between us and God. When God created us, God created us *from* God. In other words, we *are* God. Moreover, we are divine and eternal. Because we are God, we are without blemish, and we have no limitations. Our perceived separation from God is only an illusion. Separation is a lie."

I looked into her eyes and spoke calmly. "Now these beliefs are only the tip of the iceberg. Spiritual knowledge is vast. Most people on a spiritual path spend their entire lives trying to understand spiritual knowledge."

"So, I am God?" she asked quizzically. "I don't feel like God."

Chapter Eight – Federal Task Force

"You are a *part* of God and intricately connected. Thus, you are not separate from God. The source of your consciousness is from God. Everything exists within a unity of consciousness. You're not separate from anything. You don't know because you've forgotten. Now that you've been told, it will take some time to remember, if that's your destiny. Today, more and more people are remembering, and this will continue. In just a few short years, society's spiritual awareness will not even resemble what it is today."

"Because of the so-called transformation?" she asked.

I nodded.

"You said that everything is part of God," she said. "What about the devil?"

I grinned. "God is All That Is. Nothing, absolutely nothing, is not God. God is perfection and God is in perfect harmony. Everything that happens, happens with God's will. It's only our perceptions that define it otherwise. To claim that something is imperfect is to invalidate God.

"Whoa! Hold on. God is the bad guys, too? And the bad guys are perfection?"

I nodded. "The only blasphemy is the denial of God, and when you believe the bad guys are separate from God, you are denying God's existence."

The woman's eyes darted back and forth as she contemplated. After a while, she said, "Hmm, I think that I'm beginning to understand your viewpoint.

"If everything is God, then the only thing to do is to love each other, and there is no reason to judge. That's why everyone will put down their guns. The majority will realize that shooting each other is the same as shooting themselves.

She paused in contemplation. "And this same majority won't hold any anger or contempt toward those who keep shooting. They will love them, until the shooters get the

149

message that it's pointless to use violence. Eventually, this new majority will set the new rules for society."

The woman looked at me with an excited expression. "I have always believed that the only reason we have war is because two sides want to fight. If one side ever decides that fighting is pointless, then war shall cease. That's exactly what your New Age beliefs are espousing. If it didn't make so much sense, I would say that your beliefs are a dream. But if the majority believes that we are God, then anything could happen!"

She suddenly smiled brightly, and I felt the warmth in her heart. I felt as if she wanted to hug me, and she seemed much more alive now.

"*That's* what you do?" she exclaimed. "You go around and teach people that *they* are part of God?"

I grinned and nodded. "I travel a few times a year giving lectures, and I write a new book occasionally. But that's really my hobby. My real job is a restaurant owner and manager, and I have a wife and daughter who keep me busy."

She beamed joyfully. "With people like you talking about this, I can believe in the transformation. It just makes sense, and it gives me a lot more hope for this country."

We both smiled.

Chapter Nine

Final Spirit Club Meeting

I arrived back in Tucson the next morning, and Julie and Kate picked me up at the train station.

When I told Julie about my trip and experience with the FTF, she was upset, and pleaded with me to stop traveling. I told her I would sincerely think about it. However, I still had a commitment with my publisher and agent to travel and lecture.

When we arrived home, the community was having a picnic. Captain Jim was barbecuing chicken. He wore his red apron, with Captain embroidered across the chest, and his sailor's cap. This must have been a special occasion, I thought, because he didn't wear his favorite apron often.

The weather was beautiful, about 85 degrees, with a soft breeze and clear blue sky. The adults were gathered near the barbecue, sitting in chairs around canopied tables, sipping drinks and chatting. The children played nearby. The boys chased each other, and the girls sat together talking.

"What's the occasion?" I asked Julie, as we walked toward the group.

"Oh, I forgot to tell you! Captain Jim bought the park! It's ours! He bought it from the city for a million dollars. He's been trying to buy it, secretly, for months, and he got the deed last night. He didn't tell us before because he didn't want us to get our hopes up. I'm glad he didn't. Now, we just have this wonderful surprise!"

I smiled. "That's great news!"

I was now close enough to speak to the others. "Jeff, Samantha. Everyone! Good to be home. Captain, I heard the news! Now, it's really home, isn't it?"

I walked up and shook hands and hugged everyone. I thanked the Captain for his generosity and magnanimity.

"Where'd you get a million dollars?" I asked.

"I inherited some money from my parents years ago," he answered. "I turned most of it into gold coins. I was saving them for a special occasion."

"Tell me about the deed. How much land does it include? Do we have water and mineral rights? Are there any conditions?"

"The entire park is ours. All ten acres. There aren't any conditions, and we do have water rights if we want to dig a well. But I'm tapped out now, and a well will cost at least fifty-thousand dollars."

I smiled. "You did your share. Now it's up to the rest of us to get the well drilled. I think we can do it in the next few years. Wouldn't it be nice to finally have our own well?"

Everyone was in a good mood. Who cared what was going on in the world? We had each other. And now we had a place we could call home. The attitude of our community was very upbeat and optimistic. It was nice to realize that as dire as the situation was in the world, our community was persevering. We felt hopeful and we surmised there must be hope in other places throughout America.

I sat with Jeff, Samantha, and Julie. We made small talk and relished the community's good fortune. We talked about the future and what we had to do to make sure our

Chapter Nine - Final Spirit Club Meeting

community would survive. The one thing we all understood was that we had to work together as a group.

As we talked about the future, I got the urge to talk with the children. After all, they were our future. This was something that I did from time to time. The children liked hearing about spirituality and the future. Some of them considered the talks stories. Others took them to heart.

I walked over to Kevin, who was nineteen. "Kevin, gather up the kids. Time for lessons."

The twenty children, ranging in ages from five to nineteen, sat on the grass in a small group. The majority were older than ten and understood New Age spirituality better than most adults. I sat on a picnic table in front of them. They were well-behaved and sat quietly, waiting for me to begin.

"Where did we come from?" I asked them.

Several hands went up. I pointed to Lori, a ten-year-old Aquarian with an effervescent smile.

"From heaven," she said.

I nodded. "And what were you doing in heaven, Lori, before you decided to come here?"

"Planning this life. I had to decide what I wanted to do, what I needed to learn, and what I wanted to experience. I had to decide who my parents would be, and my first boyfriend." The kids snickered and laughed.

"That's right," I said. "Before we come to this planet, we plan carefully. We select our parents, our personalities, our intelligence, even the color of our eyes. So, if you have a problem, you planned it. If something happens in your life, there is a lesson there to be learned. You don't need to feel sorry for yourself. You need to recognized that you are fortunate to be here."

There was one overweight girl in the group. Her name was Jenny. One of the boys, Alex, a stimulated seven-year-old, pointed at Jenny.

"Alex, please tell Jenny why you're pointing at her."

His face turned red. "Um, I don't know."

All of the kids laughed.

"Yes, you do," I said. "You were making fun of her, weren't you?" I waited for his reply.

"Yeah, I'm sorry, Jenny," he said to her.

"Jenny, do you forgive Alex?"

"Yeah, he doesn't know any better," Jenny said. She was fourteen and mature for her age.

I nodded and continued. "We plan our lives with the intention of learning lessons. As a result, everything in our lives happens for a reason. For instance, Alex can learn from his lesson here today that it's not polite to point and make fun of people."

The younger kids snickered.

"When we judge others, we are invalidating their choices. More than that, we are invalidating their divinity. Conversely, when we accept other people's choices, we are validating their divinity." I paused.

"You mean," Jenny said, "that God doesn't care if people are overweight?"

The kids laughed.

I nodded. "Yes, that's exactly what I mean."

Jenny smiled.

I looked at Alex. "Alex, I don't mean to pick on you, so don't get mad at me. But when you make fun of somebody, you are not allowing them to have their own experiences. And don't you want to have the freedom to be yourself without anyone making fun of you?" I paused and waited for his response.

Chapter Nine - Final Spirit Club Meeting

He nodded.

"We're all equal," I continued. "It just doesn't always look that way. Everyone is God, playing a role. Do you know what a role is? It's like an actor's role in a movie. And when we plan our lives, we select the role we're going to play. Everyone has the ability to play any role. For instance, in another life you might have been a king or queen."

Everyone smiled. They had all heard me say this before, but they still reacted. They liked the concept of reincarnation.

"When you envy someone," I continued, "you probably haven't played his or her role before. So, you'll probably play that role in another life. When you loathe someone, you probably need to play that role, too."

I paused to keep the kids' attention and asked another question. "Okay, are you supposed to serve God, or do you have a choice to serve God or yourself?" A couple of hands rose. I pointed to Kevin.

"It depends on the lessons we came to learn," he said. "If we want to learn lessons about our egos, we can serve ourselves. If we want to learn lessons about love, then we serve God, which is the higher good."

"Very good answer, Kevin!" I said in a loud voice. "And if we want to learn about love, how can we serve God?"

"Well," Kevin said, "we can be grateful that God provides us with this life. By being grateful, we reduce our preoccupation with our ego. Instead, we focus more on how God is involved in our lives."

"Hmm," I said, "and how do you know if God is involved in your life?"

"Oh, God's intricately involved," Kevin said. "We just have to be aware of God's impact. Myself, I focus on God by using my intuition. I listen with my heart to what God is trying to tell me."

"Good," I said. "Does anyone have a question about this?"

Lori raised her hand. "God talks to Kevin?"

I nodded. "Of course. God talks to everyone. All you have to do is listen. However, God doesn't talk only with a voice, but also with feelings. When you feel something, sometimes that is God talking to you."

"How does God do it?" Lori asked. "How does God make us feel something?"

"By being connected to us," I said. I got up and pointed to the sky. "God created the sky. Can you imagine the creation of the sky? It's beyond our comprehension. Look at the grass and trees. God created it all. Think of the magnificence of nature. This is God's work. When you think of that magnificence, the concept of God being able to talk to everyone isn't so impossible."

Several of the children stared at the sky in contemplation. I sat back down. "God cannot create something out of nothing. Thus, if God creates something, that something is part of God. This is how we become part of God.

"We are energetic beings with an aura that surrounds our body. This aura is made up of four parts: the physical, the emotional, the mental, and the spiritual. These four parts contain a piece of our soul. Not our entire soul, only a fraction. The greater part of our soul exists in heaven, on another dimension. The fraction of our soul that surrounds our body is constantly communicating with the greater piece that is in heaven. That is how God talks to us. God is connected to our soul, which is connected to us."

I paused and looked at each of the children and Kevin, who was no longer a child. They listened attentively. They knew I would stop if they didn't pay attention.

Chapter Nine - Final Spirit Club Meeting

"When God created our souls, billions and billions of years ago, God created us as tiny replicas of God. Our souls are very much replicas of God. We are just as eternal as God, and just as perfect. We came to this planet to add experiences to our souls, and our souls add to the majesty of God. Our souls are one of the reasons the sky is so beautiful. We help God to experience beauty and to create more beauty. We are God's eyes and ears."

I paused and asked another question. "Okay, does God care what you do? Does God want you to live a certain way?"

"No," Darien, in the front row, said. She was a precocious teenager. She had been reading my books since she was nine. She and I often talked about spirituality.

"Can you explain?" I asked.

"If we're perfect," Darien said, "then why should God care? The people who care are those who want to tell everyone else how to live. God doesn't care how we live. That's what free will is all about. We get to choose our experiences and how we learn our lessons."

"Let me play devil's advocate," I said. "I want you to know that I agree with your answer, Darien. However, if God doesn't care, how come we are having so many natural disasters?"

"Well, God has this thing about harmony and balance," Darien said. "If we get too far out of balance, God steps in and changes our course. But it's not that God gets upset. God just has a natural tendency toward harmony. You might say, God forces us to love each other."

"Well said, Darien. Anybody disagree?" I asked.

"Yeah," Kevin said, "I think that God wants us to be good."

"Hmm. I can't argue with that. But do you think we should tell other people to be good? Do you think we should decide what is good, and then tell others what is acceptable?"

"Well, can't we all just agree on what is good?" Kevin asked.

"That's the problem," I said. "No, we can't. Once we start telling others what is good, we prevent the very thing we want, which is peace and harmony. Yes, I agree that God wants us to be good, but that doesn't mean we will be punished for being bad. The minute we start deciding what's good for someone else is the minute we try to play God."

I was losing some of the younger kids' interest, although the others were still attentive.

"Now, I've said that we are God. This means that we are part of God. However, we don't possess the ability to accurately decide what's good for others. We do possess the ability to decide what's good for us, and we possess the ability to get advice from God on what's good for us. Who knows what that ability is?"

A few hands went up. I pointed to Tom, a close friend of Kevin. They were sitting together in the back. "Intuition," Tom said, "the ability to know without explanation."

"Yes, intuition," I said. "Let's talk about that. Can somebody give me an example?"

Lori raised her hand. "Yesterday, Johnnie asked me to walk to Jefferson Street to get ice cream. I told him no because it's too dangerous. I had a feeling that we might get into trouble."

"Very good," I said. "Excellent example. Yes, intuition is a feeling. When you live by your feelings, your decisions don't lead you astray. In fact, you can trust your feelings. Your feelings are God talking to you."

Chapter Nine - Final Spirit Club Meeting

"Okay, last question," I said in an exaggerated, jovial manner. "When is the world going to get better?"

They all smiled. Many had been waiting expectantly for me to say, "Last question." It was my sign that they could go back to playing, and that class was almost over.

"2040," Kevin said.

"No, 2035," Jill said.

"That's too soon," Darien said.

"Why is 2035 too soon?" I asked Darien.

"Well, that's not very far away, and look at the world. Many people are changing all the time, but I can't imagine it getting better that soon. Some of the kids I talk to in town don't even know about reincarnation yet."

I looked at Jill, the girl who had said 2035. "Jill, why do you think it will be 2035?" She was eighteen and extremely aware.

"My mom says that extraterrestrials are coming. Once they reveal to the world that their spirituality matches New Age spirituality, everyone will begin to love each other. Once they begin working with us, the changes will speed up. One interesting thing is that they're going to take an interest in the New Agers, us. And when they do, other people will pay attention to how we live and what we believe."

"Good," I said. "And you think the extraterrestrials will land in public soon?"

"Yes!" Joey exclaimed. Joey was Jill's little brother. He liked to irritate her whenever he got the chance. He was nine and high-strung, and had a tremendous amount of energy. He was a Leo and liked attention. So, he was always doing things to make people react.

"Joey, that was for Jill." I turned to Jill. "Jill?"

"He's a brat," she said. "Why don't we make him wear a dunce cap?"

Several kids laughed and added their approval by clapping.

"Hmm. I don't think Joey's comment deserves the dunce cap, but we can vote. Who thinks Joey should wear the dunce cap?" I was only kidding and having fun with them.

The girls screamed, "Yeah, yeah." The boys defended Joey and booed.

"Sorry, girls. There's not enough consensus. No dunce cap for Joey."

"Joey said yes," Jill said, "because that's what I was going to say. I think they're going to land soon."

I nodded and made a face that it was possible. "All right, that's it for today."

Joey raised his hand this time, and I nodded to him.

"You didn't talk about our fake bodies," he said. "I want to hear about our fake bodies."

As usual, Joey was making us react. In this instance, he was making me react. And for double the excitement, he was forcing everyone to stay and listen to me talk about the human body. I sighed.

"Okay, but this might take a few minutes. Does everyone want to hear?"

Joey looked at everyone to imply that his feelings would be hurt if they didn't agree. Everyone stayed where they were, and nobody said no.

"Our bodies appear to be solid, but in actuality, they are just vibrating energy, and vibrating at about 100,000 cycles per second. And it's not just our bodies that are fake," I began. "Everything is an illusion: the grass, the trees, this table, our clothes, everything. Everything is energy that is vibrating at incredibly fast rates. If Jesus was here with us today, he could walk on water. How? By changing the energy structure of his body to be as light as a feather.

Chapter Nine – Final Spirit Club Meeting

"During our lifetimes, many wondrous and miraculous things will occur regarding energy transformation. The extraterrestrials will show us a few tricks, and we will learn a few of our own. Did you know that the Great Pyramid of Giza was built by changing the energy structure of the stones by using sound? The builders were able to make the huge stones float in the air.

"If you could change the energy structure of this chair," I continued, "you could make it disappear, and then laugh as I fell on the ground. But the odds of that happening are very slim, because people with this ability usually don't use it frivolously.

"Not only objects can disappear, but people can, too. There have been people born on this planet who didn't die here, and yet still left. Physical death has been bypassed by many souls. How? By changing the energy structure of the body, you can disappear. And if you can disappear, just how real is the body? Joey is correct. Our bodies are fake. The body is nothing more than a vehicle, like a suit. We use it for a lifetime, then get a new one.

"Now, it's wise to take care of the body. Why? Because the body has an intelligence of its own. I call this intelligence the innate body, and we can communicate with it. Let's talk about this next time. Today, we are out of time. The short answer today is that we can work together with the innate body to remain healthy.

I noticed that I was losing their attention. I was almost finished, however.

"Don't underestimate the intelligence of your body. Think of it as being separate from yourself. You are a soul, not a body. Think of it as your friend. And just like you treat a pet wisely, treat your body wisely. Treat your body with respect and dignity. If you take care of your body, your body will take care of you. But if you neglect the body, it will neglect you."

I paused. "Before I let you go, I want to add one last thing regarding the body. Many of you are spiritually minded and plan to pursue spiritual knowledge. Remember that health and spirituality go hand in hand. Eat nutritious food, exercise, and rest. Always listen to what your body is trying to tell you. Keep your body healthy, and it will help you with your spiritual pursuits."

I smiled as I pointed towards the park. "Okay, get out of here. That's enough for today."

The kids ran off, laughing and having fun. Some of them said thank you as they left.

* * * * *

On Wednesday night, I went to the bus station to meet Charlie, Sam, and Billy. As usual, they were waiting. When I approached, I was pleasantly surprised to see Kris with them.

"Hi, Kris. I didn't expect you to be here!" Her long, straight hair was brushed beautifully. "You look very nice."

"Thank you," she said. "Well, I figured this was the only time we could talk. You said this might be the last time you were coming."

She was right. Not only did I usually lecture and run, but this was my last trip downtown. I was turning the teaching role over to her. Julie didn't like me coming down there, and I didn't particularly like to come into that part of town.

When I first started giving these lectures, I did it because of the strange situation in which I had found myself. I didn't plan it; it just happened. Now it was time to let someone else lead.

"I'm glad you came," I said. "We can talk on the way."

Chapter Nine – Final Spirit Club Meeting

It was dark, with only the moon and various streetlights in front of us. Kris and I talked, while Charlie, Sam, and Billy led the way, ten feet ahead. Infrequently, cars drove by slowly, avoiding the random potholes in the road. Kris and I ignored the cars as we became deeply absorbed in a conversation.

"So, this is the last time you're coming to our house?" she asked.

I nodded. "Yeah, this is the last night. It's time for me to move on to other projects."

"I understand," she said, "and I don't blame you. It's dangerous to come down here, and you have a family."

Kris paused and looked at me seriously. "I'm really grateful for what you've started here, and I'll try to continue in your footsteps."

I smiled. "That's my hope ... that your *Spirit Club* will have a positive impact on the downtown community, and perhaps all of Tucson."

"Mine, too." She smiled.

"Now, what do you want to talk about?"

She looked at me cheerfully. "You carry yourself with a lot of confidence, and you seem content, as if it doesn't matter what happens tomorrow. I was wondering how you got that way."

"It's from the awareness of my divinity," I said, as we walked. "Once I realized that I was divine and literally one with God, it changed my whole perspective. For instance, why should I not be content, when I know I'm immortal? Any ideas I have of a lack of contentment come directly from my ego. This perception allows me to love myself and to love the divinity in others."

"So, you perceive yourself as a piece of God?" she asked.

I nodded. "Yes. That's exactly what I believe. More precisely, that's exactly how I feel. I feel as if my soul's immortal, and from that feeling, the only thing that makes sense is to be grateful for my life. Anything else makes no sense to me."

"Wow, that's amazing," she said.

"You can do it, too," I said. "Just ponder that you are a part of God and connected to God. Your soul is not isolated but connected to God and everything else. This is why, when you pray, God hears your prayers. Recognize your divinity, and it changes the way you think."

Kris grimaced. "It sounds easy, but I'm not there yet."

I thought for a moment. "The shortcut to spiritual awareness is recognizing your divinity. It looks as if you're going to need a few steps getting there."

"Which are?" Kris asked.

"You have to form a relationship with your higher self. You need to find out that your higher self, which is your soul, is real. This will take some practice. Start by meditating in the morning when you get up, and then keeping your mind quiet throughout the day by staying in the present moment. That silence will lead to your higher self talking to you, and you will begin to distinguish the difference between the intelligence of your ego and the intelligence of your higher self."

I paused and looked at Kris, "Does that make sense?"

She nodded, "Yeah, I think I can do that. At least I can try."

"That relationship is the starting point, or first step. Then, you have to get to the point where you perceive that life is an illusion, and that this is not our real home. That we are here on this planet to learn lessons, and then we will go home, back to heaven." I paused. "Does that make sense?"

Kris nodded.

Chapter Nine - Final Spirit Club Meeting

"Okay. When we are learning these lessons, we have to recognize that our choices have ramifications that can keep us from spiritual awareness. Thus, we have to focus on our choices and make the right ones that lead us to God. Once we realize that our choices have ramifications, we can take our spiritual path seriously. It will change from a learning exercise, to our life."

Kris looked at me as if she had an aha moment. "You mean our choices either take us closer to God or they do not? And once we are aware that our choices can bring us closer to God, that becomes our spiritual path?"

I nodded. "Exactly. For instance, addictions. These are choices that do not take us closer to God. People have addictions only because they perceive it's okay to have them. Believe me, most people love their addictions. They perceive their addictions as acceptable. We break our addictions only when we perceive them as unacceptable. And if we recognize that an addiction is unacceptable for divine awareness, we will break the addiction."

"That's what you mean by taking life seriously?" Kris asked.

I nodded. "You have to create harmony in your life, thereby creating a lifestyle that is conducive to spiritual awareness. In many respects, you have to live by virtue. You have to be true to your higher self."

"I have to become a saint?" Kris asked incredulously.

"In many respects, yes. This is the hard way to spiritual awareness. The easy way is to recognize your divinity. Then you will live like a saint automatically."

She nodded. "That makes sense."

"Kris, I've found that the best way to break addictions is to be true to your higher self. In other words, don't harm yourself. Not physically or emotionally. The first step to breaking an addiction is acknowledging that you have one. If certain actions prevent harmony in your life, then find a way to recognize why those actions exist.

"The key to finding your soul is being calm and tranquil. Have you ever noticed how calm a baby can be? Ideally, that's how you want to live. Anything that prevents that tranquility keeps you from spiritual awareness."

"Is that how you live?" Kris asked thoughtfully.

"Most of the time. There are occasions when my ego tricks me into believing I'm mortal. However, these are only lessons that bring me closer to my higher self."

"When we're calm and tranquil," I continued, "we feel love in our hearts. Conversely, when we're not, we feel anger, anxiety, or fear. It's those emotions, more than any other, that zap our harmony and disconnect our connection with our souls. Kris, live life as though you were still a child. Laugh easily. Live as if everything is a new and wonderful experience. Keep your spirit light. Even laugh at hardships. Tell yourself, in a lighthearted way, that difficulties are lessons that are bringing you closer to God. Smile at your difficulties and be grateful for the opportunity to be alive."

"So," Kris asked, "I have to create tranquility in my life, even if it doesn't always appear to be tranquil?"

I nodded. "Life is not always as it appears. Jesus was the greatest teacher, and his example is the best to follow. He could be tranquil in any situation, and so should we. As I said earlier, tranquility keeps us connected to God, whereas anxiety keeps us disconnected."

Kris looked into my eyes in deep contemplation, but didn't respond.

"The best way to deal with a tough situation," I said, "is to remain calm. You don't have to feel good about the situation, especially if there's a lot of disharmony. However,

Chapter Nine - Final Spirit Club Meeting

even in the most disharmonious situation, you can remain calm. Self-confidence, holding your power, and calmness are the way to overcome any situation. If you can harness your inner tranquility, you can overcome any situation without resorting to negative emotions.

"Feelings of frustration," I continued, "anger, anxiety, or fear are negative emotions that sap our energy. These emotions take harmony out of our lives. In other words, we create disharmony by feeling these emotions. This is the opposite of spiritual awareness. This takes us away from God. In fact, it disconnects us from God."

"I would have never thought that," Kris said. "I've always thought it was okay to get upset, if it was justifiable."

"It is okay," I replied. "It just won't take you closer to God. Spiritual awareness is a mindset. Once we get to the old soul level, we begin to perceive that, indeed, we are eternal. Once we realize this, we begin to love ourselves in a deep way. It's self-love, more than anything else, which allows us to develop a spiritual mindset. Then everything falls into place, and we find harmony in our lives.

"Kris, the only reason there isn't harmony in the world at this time is because people don't recognize their own divinity. Conversely, as more and more people recognize that they are a piece of God, the world steadily will become more harmonious. Our job is to show people their divinity. We're here to help heal their pain, to show them that their emotional pain is an illusion and that they are creating it themselves."

"Are you saying," Kris asked, "that the reason that you're calm and self-confident is that it's our natural state? In other words, you're calm because that's your *only* option?"

I looked at Kris and smiled. "Yes. Exactly. Once we perceive that we're eternal, it's only a matter of time before love and calmness become the norm in our lives. It becomes our natural way of living. There are no other options, once we truly remember who we are."

* * * * *

When we arrived at their house, it was crowded with people waiting in anticipation. The strong turnout was evidence that the people liked what they were hearing and wanted more. The teachings were having an impact. These were average people. If they accepted the messages, then the masses were ready.

I had mixed feelings. On the one hand, I was going to tell them that I wasn't coming back, and I knew this wasn't what they wanted to hear. On the other hand, I had the distinct feeling that they no longer needed me, although many may have thought they did.

Kris got everyone seated, and I began.

"I'm very excited tonight. Something has happened here that makes me feel optimistic about the world. When I began giving lectures here a month ago, few of you had been exposed to New Age spirituality. In only a few short weeks, many of you have started down a path of becoming spiritually aware."

Several people smiled warmly.

"I've been giving lectures for years, and this is the first time the messages have been accepted so quickly. Something has happened. I remember reading that the energy on the planet is changing and that, steadily, more and more people are becoming spiritually aware. I don't know if that's what has happened, but something has.

"When I give lectures, I sense the spiritual level of the audience and respond accordingly. Tonight, I feel like I can say anything, and you will understand. You're off to a fast start. It may take a year or two, but you're headed toward an

Chapter Nine - Final Spirit Club Meeting

expanded level of awareness. You're already starting to live the principles that I've been talking about."

The audience was quiet and respectful. The floor was crowded with people sitting on all available floor space. The few chairs available were taken, and many people were standing along the walls.

"Tonight is my last lecture. I'm no longer needed here. You're well on your way. Kris has agreed to continue holding the meetings every week. She is going to take my place. Honor her for her courage. I'm sure she will do a great job, if you allow her."

Many people looked at Kris with a surprised look on their faces.

"So, keep coming on Wednesday nights. Bring New Age literature and share it. Begin reading. That's the best way to learn. Talking among yourselves also will help, but seek out and expose yourself to New Age knowledge.

"You'll find plenty of New Age literature in Tucson. Arizona is at the heart of the New Age movement. After a few months of reading and sharing your ideas, you might want to take a pilgrimage to Sedona, or to Black Mesa to visit with the Hopi, or another place to which you are drawn.

"Like I said, I'm excited. Even if you don't realize it yet, I can see that you're going to create positive changes. You are the masses. I might be a spark, but it's people like you who create real change. Once enough people change their beliefs, the world will change."

I paused to see if everyone understood the impact they could generate.

"We are living during a monumental period of history," I added with emphasis. "What is happening here is the beginning of the New Age. By the end of the decade, thousands of small groups like yours will be forming and spreading these ideas. It will be small groups like yours that started the trend." I smiled.

"By 2050, the New Age movement will have flourished to such an extent that anger and violence will be isolated events, on their way to near extinction. Anger and violence will be replaced by love and a sense of humanity. We're going to create a paradise. And by the year 2050, the next civilization will have formed its nascent beginning. The next 20 years will be the birth of a new civilization, and you get to be the progenitors.

"I have been expecting signs to start appearing, and your group is the best sign I've come across." They smiled. "I know that there are many spiritual groups all over the country, but most of them have been formed by New Agers. Yours is the first group I've come across that was formed strictly by word of mouth, and by people with very little exposure to New Age knowledge."

Many in the audience murmured and applauded themselves.

"Your group came together spontaneously. It just happened. You were searching for answers, and I just happened to be here. Two or three years ago, most of you would have stayed away. You were still clinging to your old beliefs. Now that the world has changed so dramatically, you recognize that new beliefs are required.

"It's time to create a new civilization," I continued. "And you're looking for direction. If my messages didn't ring true, you would have kept searching elsewhere."

I sighed. "Well, this is my last lecture. So, let's get started. To be honest, I didn't know what I was going to talk about tonight, and I still don't know. I'll just open my mouth and see what comes out."

They laughed.

Chapter Nine - Final Spirit Club Meeting

"Life should be effortless," I said. "If what you're doing isn't effortless, then you're doing something wrong. Right now, I'm letting words flow effortlessly. This is how our lives should be.

"In each instant, we should be tuned into what God, and we, have planned for our lives. Intuitively, we should know what lessons we came to learn. When we're tuned in to those lessons, each moment of our lives is effortless.

"When we struggle, it's a sign that change in our lives is required to find a new path. The only purpose of frustration is to point to another choice that is available. If we're frustrated, we can perceive the frustration as something we created in order to lead us down a different path...."

A lady in front interrupted. She was in her thirties, with very short hair and a calm serenity. "Are you implying that we should try to create our own lives?"

"You are creating your own life," I said. "Everything that happens in your life, you are creating. The key is in perceiving *how* you are creating it. Perception is everything. The very meaning of life is to learn perception, and to become more spiritually aware.

"Perception, awareness, and even knowledge are learned by the soul, and not by the mind. When we leave this body, we leave the mind behind, but we take the soul with us."

I paused, but the lady did not reply, so I went on.

"If life isn't effortless," I continued, "something is askew. It's okay for our lives not to be effortless. There's nothing wrong with struggle and frustration. If these conditions are prevalent in your life, these are your lessons. These are also your signs that something spiritual is missing from your life, and that another path is available."

A woman raised her hand, and I pointed to her. "Are you saying that work should be effortless, too?"

I nodded. "If you accept it as what you have chosen to do, as your creation, then you should not resist it. The only thing that prevents work from being effortless is resistance. Once you become spiritually aware, this resistance should fade. This is why Gandhi smiled when they handed him a mop in prison. He had no resistance."

I turned my attention back to the entire group.

"Okay," I said, "let's switch to fear. Be as fearless as you can. I know it's difficult to be fearless all the time, but be fearless as much as possible. Instead of living in fear, try to live in trust. Live each day as an opportunity for learning the lessons you came to learn…"

"What if I don't like the lessons?" interrupted a lady on the crowded floor.

I smiled at her. "Then change them, or if you can't change them, learn to live with a sense of gratitude. One of these choices is always possible, because spiritual awareness is not impossible to obtain. You can become more aware, which can lead to your well-being."

She nodded.

"There are a few things that help us with fear," I said to the group. "First, recognize that all of the events in your life are planned. Second, realize that all of the events in your life happen for a reason, and that the world is divinely ordered. From this perspective, allow these events into your life without resistance. Trust God.

"We fear because we don't trust. If we had perfect trust that God was watching out for us, we would have very little, if any, fear. However, as I have said previously, this planet is very dense, which makes it difficult to perceive our connection to God.

"Another thing we can do about fear is to detach from a stressful experience and ask ourselves why it is happening.

Chapter Nine - Final Spirit Club Meeting

Instead of quickly jumping to conclusions, and becoming afraid, analyze the situation objectively. If you detach your emotions from the situation and remain calm, you'll limit your fear, if not actually prevent it."

"I don't understand," said a teenager standing along the wall. "When you say detach, do you mean, like a daydream?"

I smiled. "Yeah, it is like daydreaming. When a traumatic event occurs, try to detach from your current environment. Instead, put your awareness outside of your conscious mind, like in a daydream, and become aware of why it's occurring, and why you created it."

I looked at the young teenager with awe, smiling again. "Great idea. Thanks for the input."

He smiled and nodded.

"To eliminate fear," I said, "realize that all events are created for a purpose. Think in terms of how God perceives a situation. To God, all events are the result of our beliefs. In other words, God is a detached spectator, watching our lives unfold, although God is also intricately involved.

"God is not only a spectator, but is also running the show. It's complicated, and our limited awareness makes it nearly impossible to understand. In a nutshell, there's nothing to fear, because God is indeed watching out for us. Everything that happens in our lives happens because God *wants* it to happen. This is God's show. We're all actors playing roles, and God is in charge of the play. God's the director.

"When we perceive fear," I continued, "it is because we can't perceive God. As I said before, we perceive fear only because we don't trust that God is watching out for us. Have you noticed how people call out God's name when they need help? If they had trust, they would know it isn't necessary to call God, because God is already present.

"Not only is God always present, but God doesn't perceive there is a problem that needs to be rectified. As far as God is concerned, all situations are perfect. God doesn't create imperfect experiences. I know this can be difficult to grasp, but until we do, we will live in fear. The very belief that evil exists is enough to create evil. Thus, if we believe in evil, we have a reason to be afraid. For, God will reveal to us whatever we believe."

I paused and scanned the room. "When we find God, our focus turns away from us and toward the big picture, which is humanity. When we find God, our desire switches from us and toward God. This happens automatically, as we become aware that everything is interrelated.

"As our awareness increases, it becomes increasingly untenable to focus on ourselves. We become aware of the greater forces in life. It gets to the point where we realize it's fruitless to focus on ourselves. We literally say to ourselves, 'Humanity is much more important than my personal lifestyle.' At that point, we begin to live in harmony with humanity."

Kris, seated on the floor a few feet away, asked, "Are these forces our guardian angels?"

I looked at her. "They can be. These forces include guardian angels, spirit guides, our higher selves, and God. Everyone's lives are impacted continuously from the higher planes. The concept of free will is an illusion. We have free will only to make choices that are in agreement with these forces. We have many choices, however, to a large extent, they are restricted by the larger forces in our lives."

I paused and looked at Kris. "This is a big topic, and I can't explain it in only a few minutes. This is something you are going to have to research and share with the group."

I smiled, and she smiled back.

Chapter Nine - Final Spirit Club Meeting

I looked back to the group. "Do you see the difference between focusing on yourself versus focusing on humanity? Being spiritual and not being spiritual are like night and day. There's a big difference. People who focus primarily on themselves aren't ready to search for the truth. They are so caught up in their own ego desires that the concepts of spirituality elude them.

"I'll end with another statement by Ram Dass. He said that we have to be careful what we say to non-spiritual people. Why? Because they think their personalities and identities are real. In other words, they have a vested interest in their identities. Anything that threatens this belief will be met with resistance.

"I tell you this because, if you try to initiate new believers, you can expect resistance for this reason. What you're going to be doing is trampling on some very fragile egos. Don't get upset if your group stays fairly small and many people ignore you for this reason.

"I have a feeling that you make up the majority of old souls in the downtown area. You were all drawn here. I'm sure there are more people in the area who will join your group, but don't expect everyone to be open to these concepts."

I paused. "I hope that everything goes well. I'll stop by sometime in the next month or so. Thank you for having me." I bowed.

The audience applauded, and it was over. I shook hands and hugged several people. Kris and I had an emotional goodbye.

Then Charlie, Sam, and Billy walked me back to the bus station. As we said farewell, I noticed their demeanor had changed from the first time we had met. They were no longer belligerent. In fact, I had the distinct impression that from now on, they were going to be nice guys. I wouldn't be surprised if they began keeping the peace down here.

"Wow," I thought, "the New Age has arrived."

Chapter Nine - Final Spirit Club Meeting

www.ingramcontent.com/pod-product-compliance
Lightning Source LLC
Chambersburg PA
CBHW071922290426

44110CB00013B/1442